Metal Butterfly

✦

"Lupus, the enemy that lurked within me"

Jennifer De Sousa

iUniverse, Inc.

New York Lincoln Shanghai

Metal Butterfly
"Lupus, the enemy that lurked within me"

iUniverse books may be ordered through booksellers or by contacting:

iUniverse
2021 Pine Lake Road, Suite 100
Lincoln, NE 68512
www.iuniverse.com
1-800-Authors (1-800-288-4677)

Because of the dynamic nature of the Internet, any Web addresses or links contained in this book may have changed since publication and may no longer be valid.

The views expressed in this work are solely those of the author and do not necessarily reflect the views of the publisher, and the publisher hereby disclaims any responsibility for them.

ISBN: 978-0-595-43281-3 (pbk)
ISBN: 978-0-595-87622-8 (ebk)

Printed in the United States of America

Metal Butterfly

God
Bless),
Jennifer DeSiva

This is dedicated first and
foremost to God who has helped
me every bit of the way. My parents, sisters,
family, and friends who have made my life what it is today.

A percentage of the proceeds will be dedicated
to the Lupus Foundation, and Breast Cancer Society in
remembrance of my mother and I whom have defeated these
terrible diseases, hoping that someday there will be a cure
and a resolution.

I would also like to thank my employer, Prima Care PC in Fall
River for helping me carry out my message to everyone, and for
helping me when I was facing the worst moments of my life.

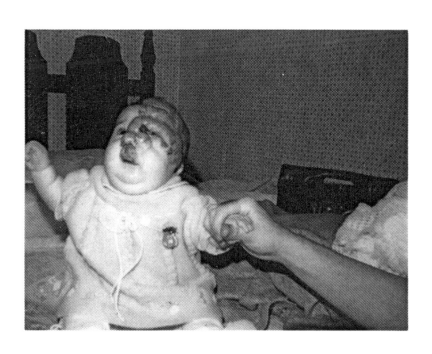

Contents

Dear Reader,

This story about my life, disguised as Miss Jennifer Wright was an emotional, and extraordinary journey. My life was filled with suffering and pain but, beneath my challenges, I've never lost hope in living a normal life like any human being.

At birth I was born with a Hemangioma, and as I grew the benign blood tumor also grew. It had spread down the left side of my face leaving me with no vision on my left eye, and also leaving me with a disfigured appearance. As a baby I suffered because, the Hemangioma would cause me so much pain. Sometimes it would rupture, and I'd have to be taken to the hospital.

When I turned seventeen, I almost died in Lisbon, Portugal due to Renal Failure, and Congestive Heart Failure caused by Systemic Lupus Erythematosus (SLE). After that major flare, once in a while I'd have small flares. However, my sickness was manageable and under control.

In the year of 2005, I had another major flare. It once more triggered my lungs, heart, and kidneys. My kidneys this time completely shutdown, and I had to plan my life around dialysis. After about a year of doing dialysis three times a week, my kidneys miraculously improved. Doctors just couldn't understand how my kidney function could've improved so much. I had started off with End Stage Renal Failure, and was now with almost all of my kidney function back. My only answer to their questions was that, it was done by the power of God.

Out of my experience, I've become one strong person. I don't let anything bother me, or get in my way. Life is too short and too precious to waste. I live life to the fullest, and when my enemy calls, I defeat every bit of it and let it know that I am stronger.

Sincerely,

Jennifer De Sousa

1

Newborn

At 1:16 in the morning of June 10, 1982, Miranda Wright my mother, gave me birth. My father Andrew, stood by my mother's side as she held me in her arms for the very first time, and smiled at both of us. My parents at that moment decided to call me Jennifer Wright. I was a healthy 6 lbs. and 11oz baby that cried just like every other baby in that nursery but, there was something I had that the others didn't have. I had a little birthmark on my forehead that looked like a bruise.

Later in the day when the nurse brought me in my mother's room, my parents questioned her about the birthmark, and told her they wanted to speak with my mother's obstetrician. I was my mother's first, and my parents were concerned. The nurse gladly paged the doctor, and in an hour or so Dr. Pedrotty arrived.

My parents thought that the obstetrician was at fault for me having this birthmark because, I was taken out with iron forceps during the delivery. The only thing my parents could think of was that maybe the doctor had hurt me when he took me out. My parents argued back and forth with the doctor but, the truth was that no one was at fault, and no one knew how, and why I ended up being born with this birthmark. I guess it was just a sign of a first challenge for my parents and I to face.

My parents didn't know what else to think but, to leave it in God's hands hoping that it wouldn't turn out to be anything critical. When I went home, as the days passed by, my bruise started turning pinkish, and started spreading down the left side of my face catching the left side of my nose and left eye keeping it shut. A few days later it started getting red, and I'd cry constantly because I was always in so much pain. My parents were in panic, and called my Pediatrician. When my Pediatrician looked at my face, he knew that my case was severe, and that I was going to need immediate treatment. He referred me to Children's Hospital for a consultation, and told my parents that there were great doctors at Children's Hospital who could take care of me in the best manner.

That night while I was playing in my crib, all of a sudden blood started gushing out of my face. As blood covered my face, I kept screaming until my mother walked in. My mother was panic. She stopped the bleeding by using a diaper against my face, and then called my father at work. She called my Pediatrician in morning, and I was sent by emergency call to Children's Hospital.

I was seen by a Plastic Surgeon named Edward Holmes, who was familiar with these very few cases like mine. The first thing he told my parents was that it wasn't cancerous. Then he explained to my parents that what I had was called a Hemangioma. He also told us that a Hemangioma is like a clump of abnormal blood vessels that in most cases is caused by blood disorders. It's a benign tumor of blood vessels that grows within time and may in severe cases double its original size or even greater than that.

"How could my daughter have caught this?" My mother asked the doctor.

Dr. Holmes told us that at least one out of fifty babies is born with a Hemangioma, and that the only concrete evidence they have is that it runs in the family. He asked my parents if there was anyone in the family who had a blood disorder but according to my parents' knowledge, in our family no one had a blood disorder. He basically stated that my Hemangioma was genetically inherited but, from where?

My maternal grandmother had Rheumatoid Arthritis, and my paternal grandmother had Diabetes. My grandfather's were healthy except for my paternal grandfather who had asthma. There was no link between these diseases and my disorder.

After a moment of thought, Dr. Holmes made an assumption. He told us that this disorder could be caused by an autoimmune disease that may progress as I get older. In one way it fit the category because, both my grandmothers had autoimmune diseases.

Dr. Holmes also stated that girls are more prone to be born with this disorder especially, those with fair, or lighter skin like me. He also stated that most likely it would stop growing after six months but, in my case it grew beyond what was expected. My left eye was completely shut due to the Hemangioma that had spread down the left side of my face, and that left side was totally disfigured. Because my left eye was shut due to the Hemangioma, it couldn't fully develop. My doctor told my parents that I may become legally blind from my left eye, and that glasses for safety precautions would be appropriate when I get older to protect my right eye.

The main treatments of choice they used to prevent the growth of this benign tumor were oral corticosteroids such as, Prednisone to stop the growth until the Hemangioma was in its quiescent stage. My doctor put me on Prednisone, and also warned my parents that this treatment would probably stunt my growth. However, all that mattered to my parents was my health.

Dr. Holmes told my parents that when I become older, constructive plastic surgery and laser treatment would be an opinion. The laser treatment would simply remove the redness of the Hemangioma known as, "port wine stains." My parents kept listening very carefully and attentively to what the doctor had to say with total trust that this doctor was going to do what was best for me. They had no where else to turn except trusting in these doctors.

Before we left, a nurse came in and explained to my mother how to treat the ulcerations around my left eye lid, and open wounds I had from previous blood vessel rupturing. The nurse told my mother that this treatment needed to be done in order to prevent scarring. The instructions seemed straight forward to my mother but, deep down in her heart all she could think of was how painful it was going to be on me.

As we headed back home, my parents were very quiet. They were both dwelling on their own thoughts and concerns. After a while when I was almost asleep, my mother started talking,

"Why did this happen to us? Why!?" My mother cried.

"I don't know, honey! I don't know!" My father answered.

Every night when my mother came in with a basin filled with water and a first aid kit, I knew it was for torture. She'd place wet face cloths on my ulcerations, and open wounds. Then after half-hour or so, she'd pull the cloths out to take all the dried blood and bacteria that were harvesting there. I would scream with so much pain, and my mother would cry a river. She hated doing this to me but, she knew it was for my sake.

I was a lucky person, I have to say. I had wonderful parents who loved me tremendously. They didn't reject me because, I was sick. Instead, they suffered along with me because they truly loved me.

In one way, this episode in our life brought us together. It made my parents stronger human beings, and made them more united, unlike in the being of their marriage when my father would spend his weekend at a bar close to home to chit chat with his buddies instead of being home with my mother.

When all these problems with me came about, he realized that his presence at home was more important. My father loved my mother, and wanted to be there to support her through these tough moments. He needed her as much as she needed him to overcome all of this.

This was my mother's first child! Her first child! If you were a newly wed couple, and gave birth to a sick child, how would you feel? It's not easy. Every time my mother played with me, I knew that in the back of her mind she was constantly worrying about me. Worrying if I was in pain. Worrying about my future, and most of all worrying if I would someday fit in with everyone else without being picked on. It broke both my mother and father's hearts to see me suffer silently when I couldn't cry anymore.

In the very few times I wasn't in pain, I'd value my time and play with my toys. I would especially play with my pink and blue teddy bear that I called my "Friend." I was a very happy little girl when I wasn't in pain. I'd enjoy every pain-free moment I had to the fullest, and valued my time.

My parents brought me to Children's Hospital every two weeks for a consultation with my doctor. After my Hemangioma seemed to be quiescent due to the Prednisone I was taking, I started making once a month visits to my doctor. Then I ended up just going every six months, and so on. My parents were pleased with my doctor's advice, and were fascinated with his work when my doctor had shown them pictures of babies with Hemangiomas, and their progress over the years after constructive plastic surgery. My parents agreed that when I get older this would be one of the best things they could ever do for me. It would make me look like a normal child, and would make me feel much better about myself in the long run.

My mother worked as a teller for Bank of New England but because I needed to be taken care of, she had to quit. Money was tight but, they managed for my sake. Everywhere my parents went, they'd bring me. I was their child and they weren't ashamed of that.

It didn't matter to them that I was different from other children. That didn't change anything. They loved me for whom I was.

However, sometimes outsiders were very rude and ignorant. I loved going out with my parents but, I could never go anywhere without being constantly stared at. It felt so uncomfortable to leave the house knowing that wherever I went, people would stare. Some would literally stop, and stare at me as if I were some kind of monster.

One day this old Portuguese lady stopped next to my mother's carriage, then looked at my mother, and gave her a nasty look.

"How could you come out with this child?" The old lady asked my mother.

My mother wasn't stupid! She knew what that old lady wanted to say. She wanted to tell my mother that she should be ashamed of walking out of the house with me. That's what the old hag wanted to say.

My mother faced the old woman.

"She's my daughter, and I love her."

The old lady didn't know what to say, and ended up leaving with such disgrace. My mother then looked at me, and began to cry.

"I don't care what people say about you. I love you, Jennifer and will never abandon you." My mother told me.

"Mama. Don't cry. I love you too." I smiled.

When we came home that day, my father was watching television and noticed that my mother was upset. He turned off the television, and started helping her with the groceries.

"What's wrong? You seem so quiet." He asked.

"Oh. It's just some stupid old lady I meant at the grocery store." My mother tried brushing it off.

"Why is she stupid? May I ask?"

"It's nothing. I'm ok. Really, I am."

"No. You're not ok! You look like you've been hurt. What did that old hag tell you?" My father was concerned.

My mother sat down on the kitchen chair, and began crying. My father then kneeled down to her level.

"Tell me. What's wrong? You can trust in me."

"I'm just upset about what this old Portuguese lady told me at the grocery store about our little girl." She told him as she looked into his eyes.

"Why? What did that old hag tell you?" My father asked.

"She questioned me about how I could go out with our daughter in public. I knew what she meant! She was trying to tell me that our daughter is some kind of monster that shouldn't be seen in public! That's exactly what she meant!" My mother told my father with such agony.

"That old hag! I wish I was there because, I would've told her where to go!" My father was furious. He wasn't going to let anyone talk like that about his family.

After my mother wiped her tears, she ran her fingers through my daddy's hair and gave him a kiss on his forehead. Once my father lifted his head and gave her those luscious eyes, I realized that it was time I minded my own business. I ended up going to my room and played with my toys as I talked to my "Friend."

"I think mommy and daddy are in love. What do you think?" I asked my "Friend."

My growth progress was very slow due to the high dosage of Prednisone I was taking but, my brain was intact and I was one smart cookie. I enjoyed learning and experiencing new things, and also loved watching television. For me, T.V. was like a school of knowledge where I was introduced to so many different things.

After three years of marriage saving and sacrificing, my parents decided to buy a cottage in Westport. It was a nice quiet property with quite a bit of land. The house had two bedrooms, a living room, dining room, a kitchen, an extra storage room that my mother turned into a guest room, and there was also a big basement. As time moved on, little by little my parents worked on remodeling the house. They put new cabinets in the kitchen, turned the basement into a bar and entertainment area, and had new siding be put on the house.

Sometimes I was scared to be in my room by myself at night, and would call my mother from my room, as I covered myself with the blankets of my crib.

"Mommy! Mommy!" I cried.

"What's wrong, sweety?" My mother asked as she came into my room.

"There's a monster that crawls up my window when you're not here! I'm afraid, mommy!"

"There's nothing to be afraid of, sweety. There are no monsters here."

"Can I sleep with you, mommy?" I asked.

"Of course!" My mother replied.

My mother didn't mind because, my father wasn't home. He worked third shifts at a textile factory, and was never home for the nights except on his days off. There was always plenty of room for me. However, I was a bed hog. Many times when my mother and I woke up, she'd be on the edge, and I as small as I was, would practically be in the middle of the bed.

I could tell my mother dreaded getting up on Saturday's because, it was a cleaning day.

"God. Why couldn't you have made the night last longer? I feel like I've just gotten in bed. Give me strength!" She'd say every Saturday morning. After her little prayer, she always stood lying down in bed for a while deep in her thoughts. I'd slip out of the room quietly and go to the guest room to play while she remained in bed. When she'd finally get up, she'd always check on me and every time she looked at me, she always had a bright smile. Her smiles always made me feel so good.

"Good morning!" She'd tell me.

"Good morning, mommy!" I'd reply as I'd give her a hug and kiss.

She then would bring me to the kitchen, and make my favorite for breakfast. Pancakes. After washing the dishes, my mother would bring me into the living room, and put the television on so she could get her housework done. My favorite show called the "Smurf's" gave every Saturday morning. Anytime there was something giving on television that I liked to watch, I'd get so happy and would start dancing and prancing with my "Friend." Already as an infant, I learned to appreciate the little things life has to offer. I suffered too much to be spoiled or greedy. I became content with what my parents could give me, and to me their love and care were all I needed.

When my father came home from work every Saturday mornings, as my mother vacuumed, he'd ask her for it and then would go after me with it. He'd take the long cone-shaped vacuum, and would chase me in the living room with it as he raised and maneuvered it at the same time. I would get so scared of the loud noise from the vacuum, and would start crying. Then I would run with all my might to the guest room, and close myself in there every time. I was afraid of the vacuum especially because, my father made me feel like I was going to be sucked up when he'd chase me and raise it at the same time. After a minute or two, I'd open the door very slowly and peek to see if the horrifying vacuum was still in site to catch me. When I'd see that all was clear, I would go back into the living room to play. My parents, especially my dad would laugh so much to see my reaction when I'd get all scared, and frightened. He loved to see me get all panicked.

I used to hate when my mother made baked beans for dinner because, I didn't like them. I didn't like the look, the smell or the taste. My mother always tried to make me eat them but, I refused every time.

"Eat your beans, Jennifer!" My mother would tell me.

"I don't like them, and I won't eat what I don't like!" I'd firmly reply.

"Jennifer! You're not getting up from this table until you eat those beans." She'd tell me.

"Fine!" I'd tell her. Because of my stubbornness, I'd end up sleeping beside my plate of baked beans, every time she made them for dinner. When morning came, my mother would head to the kitchen and find me practically drooling on the kitchen table beside my plate of baked beans.

"Wake up! You are so stubborn! Why don't you like my beans?" She'd get all upset.

"They're gross!" I'd make an ugly face.

"They're healthy!" My mother would reply.

"I don't care. I won't eat what I don't like!" I'd reply.

Then with that remark, I'd close myself in the guest room because I knew I was being a bad girl. When I'd close the door every time, I'd encounter that horrifying vacuum that was hidden in back of the door, and would start screaming as I'd run to my mother.

"See! You should've eaten the beans. Maybe you wouldn't be so afraid of the vacuum." My mother would tell me.

My parents had such a big basement that they called their cellar. Down there they had a big bar and a stereo for parties, and company. Every weekend my mother's sisters would come over, and do aerobics. I wanted to be a part of it too and so, I would try imitating the exercises my mother and aunts would do. I was only four years of age, and forced my mother to include me on the chart profile she created with everyone's weight. I was a chubby forty pounds but, that didn't stop me from doing all the exercises my family was doing. Every week I looked at that chart, and would bring it up to my mother.

"Mom. Am I losing weight?"

"No, sweety. You don't need to lose weight!"

"Yes, I do." I always insisted.

The following week I'd try harder in my aerobics sweating profusely with my lips all bunched together expressing myself with a tough look.

On Sunday's my grandfather, my mother's father would come and visit us, and every Sunday I would pull my grandfather's arm for him to go downstairs to the cellar, and dance the chicken song with me. I loved dancing the chicken song with my grandfather. It was a way to bond a little.

Sometimes when it was a good day outside, my mother would take me outside and swing me on a tire that was tied to a big tree that was in front of the house. My parents only earned a minimum wage of four dollars an hour, and they couldn't afford luxury but, for me it didn't seem to matter because anything made me happy. We also had a lot of rabbits on our land because, we were surrounded by woods. I'd get all happy when I'd see a rabbit, and would try chasing it but never had any luck catching one.

My mother had gone back to work when I was a little older, and used to leave me with my great-grandmother. My great-grandmother Helena, was an old-fashioned lady born in St. Michael's, Azores. Her husband Manuel was also born in St. Michael's, Azores, and had served the Vietnam War for a while. At that time Helena took her role as a domestic housewife taking care of her five children. She had two boys, and three girls. Helena had no schooling when she was a kid because, back then only the rich or those who could offer chickens, and goods to the faculty could attend school in the Azores. She couldn't read or write, and depended on her husband to take care of things that involved reading and writing. As a wife she kept the house clean and cozy, and did the cooking. When Helena's eldest daughter was about three years of age, she passed away due to a heart attack. It happened when Helena had gone to a mini mart store close by, and brought her daughter with her so she wouldn't walk by herself. For some reason, her daughter was behind, and then all of a sudden she hears,

"Moo." "Moo."

It was a mad cow that escaped from one of the pasture's close by, and was heading her way. Her poor little heart started beating so fast, that she suddenly passed out. You'd think it was just simple fainting, but no! This was serious. She had a heart attack, and died right there.

After the war was over, Helena and Manuel decided to go live in America. They knew that in America they could have better lives with more abundance. America was always known as the land of freedom and opportunity.

I was Helena's first great-granddaughter, and she loved me very much. She'd order some special cremes, and lotions to put on my Hemangioma to see if it would go away, and would pray every day beside me while I took my afternoon nap as she'd rub the creme on my lesions.

When I'd wake up from my nap, my great-grandmother would call me into the kitchen, and pour me a nice bowl of Portugese soup. The soup was made with chicken broth, spinach, pieces of chicken, macaroni, beans, and pieces of carrot and potato. She would also add salt, and pepper to give the final touch. I loved it so much that I'd leave the bowl spotless.

Every Saturday my great-grandparents would pick me up, and bring me to mass with them. When they both took care of me, they'd go out shopping with me sometimes. However, every time they took me out shopping they'd have to keep a close eye on me because, I had the habit of playing hiding go seek. My great-grand-father loved to drive. Many times he would travel to different kinds of beaches to catch quahogs, and drive to Canada to see family but, when he approached his 60's his legs gave up on him. He could no longer drive, and could only walk with a cane.

2

Growing Up

I was growing up so fast, and my entire family was proud of my progress. I considered myself normal like everyone else, and learned to become one tough cookie who stood up for herself. However, I was always surrounded by family and that's what kept me going.

When I turned five, I was supposed to start school but, my parents were afraid. They were afraid that I was going to get picked on because of my birth defect.

"I don't want our daughter going to school and coming home crying every day because, some kid made fun of her!" My father argued.

"She has to go, honey! We can't make her feel like she's different from everyone else." My mother replied.

"We'll hold her back this first year. Next year if we feel more comfortable about sending her to school, we'll register her. Ok?" My father replied.

"Ok." My mother replied as she grabbed my father's bottom lip with hers.

My father then grabbed hers and whispered,

"I love you, Miranda."

"I love you too, Andrew. Watch. Jennifer is going to do just fine in school, and I can bet you that she is going to make many friends."

Well. I guess you can say, I was a bit nosy but after that little romantic fling, I covered my eyes, and ran to my room. If they knew that I was listening to their conversation, I'd be chopped liver. The first thing my mother would do, would be to chase me with the broom. My father only had to use his loud voice, and just that was enough to make me cry.

We had lived in our cottage for about three years, and my parents were now deciding to sell it to make profit. In those three years economy had a boost, and pricing increased. With this, a minimum wage was extended to six dollars an hour to make the cost of living affordable. When my parents sold their house, they had made almost double of what they paid for it. What were they going to do with all this money? Good question.

My father was born in Terceira, Azores, and so was his sisters and parents. He and his family always dreamed of going back to their homeland, and make a living there. The reason why my father and his family had come to America, was to make some money so they could go back and live out there comfortably.

My father had the same dream of going back. However, my mother wasn't that thrilled of leaving her homeland, and moving somewhere where she didn't know anyone except my father and his family. Her homeland was here and besides, she couldn't speak the language very well. Despite my mother's contradiction about moving to the Azores, my father was her husband. She wanted to make him happy, and had agreed in conquering his dream.

We moved into my great-grandmother's apartment houses up to the third floor and spent five years of our lives sacrificing, saving and buying things to bring with us to the Azores for the dream house my parents were constantly sketching.

When I turned six, my parents decided to register me in school. My mother's friend named Sharon, who worked with her at Bank of New England, also had a son that was going to start school too.

Sharon helped my mother get me registered at the same school her son was going to attend, that way I would feel more comfortable because, I'd have at least one friend. With this, my mother felt more comfortable and didn't worry as much about sending me to school.

A few days before school sessions started for the Kindergarten class at Coughlin School, my mother made an appointment to talk with my teacher, Mrs. Rhoda Perkins. When we first meant Mrs. Perkins, we were a bit intimidated. She had a very tall and slim figure, and her face was practically hidden by all of her black blotchy hair that draped from side to side, with bangs that covered her dark brown eyebrows. Despite her appearance, Mrs. Perkins was a very nice, and caring teacher.

"Good morning, Miranda and Jennifer Wright." Mrs. Perkins welcomed us.

"Good morning, Mrs. Perkins. This is my daughter Jennifer who will be attending your class this year." My mother replied.

"You have a beautiful daughter, Mrs. Wright."

"Thanks." My mother replied.

"May I ask you Mrs. Wright, what happened to Jennifer?"

"That's why I'm here Mrs. Perkins. When Jennifer was born, she had a little bruise on her forehead and as she grew, the bruise became larger. It had spread from her forehead down to her left eye keeping it shut, and also the left side of her nose. She is legally blind from her left eye because of it being shut for so long. However, her right eye is perfectly normal. She's being followed up with a Plastic Surgeon at Children's Hospital, and he told us she has a Hemangioma, which is a blood vessel tumor."

"Is it cancerous?" My teacher asked.

"No. It's due to abnormal blood vessels." My mother replied.

"Poor thing. Boy! Mrs. Wright, you must have a huge load on your shoulders." "Tell me about it! Have you ever heard of that phrase? The faithful receive the challenges, and the betrayers receive the blessings?"

"Oh, Miranda don't think of it that way. Blessings will come your way. Sometimes God tests our faith" My teacher preached.

"I'm just concerned that kids may pick on, or make fun of Jennifer because of her birth defect."

"Oh don't worry Mrs. Wright. I will introduce Jennifer to her new friends, and will explain to them why she has that birth defect. Watch, they're all going to love her."

"So, Miss Jennifer! Are you excited about starting school?" My teacher asked me.

"Yeah! I know how to write my name." I proudly replied.

"Well, that's a good start!" My teacher smiled at me.

"Thanks for your comforting words, Mrs. Perkins." My mother said.

"You're always welcome." My teacher replied.

"Ok, Jennifer. We're going to leave. Say goodbye to Mrs. Perkins." My mother told me.

"Bye." I said as I waved my left hand.

"Goodbye, sweetie. See you in class next week." My teacher replied.

The days seemed to fly by, and my first day of school came sooner than expected for me and my parents. My mother dressed me in a lilac dress that had pink flowers embedded on the cotton fabric. The dress looked just perfect on me. Although I had that defect on my face, I always looked pretty.

"Ready?" My mother asked.

"Yeah!" I replied with so much excitement.

When I arrived with my mother, we went right to the classroom. All of my classmates were sitting on the floor in a circle, and there was one available spot designated for me to complete the circle. My teacher would call it the circle of friendship.

"Come in my dear!" Mrs. Perkins said.

"Kids, this is Jennifer who will also be part of our class. Many of you may be wondering why she has a defect on her face. Jennifer was sick when she was a baby and that's why she has this defect. However, I can tell you that she is a normal child like everyone else, and is very sweet. Please welcome Jennifer into our circle of friendship with a strong round of applause!"

I felt so special. After I smiled to everyone, I sat down beside two of my new friends with so much excitement. Then I glanced at my mother, and all of the other mothers that were lined up ready to leave their sons and daughters for their first day of class. My mother was crying. She had taken care of me constantly due to sickness, sheltered and protected me from harm and because of this, she became very attached to me. I could tell that she was worried about introducing me to the outside world. She always had that fear that I was going to be picked on. She didn't want that happy little girl I was, turn out to be miserable and unhappy. My health condition had given me enough problems to face in my life, and I didn't need anything else to bring me down.

I enjoyed my first day of school. All of my classmates were very understanding, and played with me like any other child. I wasn't left out.

"Mommy, I made a lot of friends today!" I told my mother when she picked me up after my first day of school.

"I'm happy you did!" My mother smiled at me.

The second day wasn't as good as the first. My classmates weren't the one's who ruined my day. It was the others. The other students would constantly pick on me, and make fun of me when I'd go outside on my recess break.

"Look at that monster." They'd laugh.

"She has a cherry nose." A boy chuckled.

I'd get so heartbroken, and would cry silently sitting on one of the school steps that lead to the entrance. One day this boy from my class approached me as I stood crying with my hands covering my face as I sat on one of the steps.

"What's wrong?" This boy from my class asked.

"Some kids were making fun of me. They say I look like a monster." I wept.

"Don't listen to them, Jennifer. They don't know what they say. I don't know if you remember me but, I'm in your class. My name is Scotty, and you can play with me if you want."

I smiled, and wiped my tears. That was so sweet of him. He was so caring, and I liked that. From that day on, Scott and I were constantly together. We would play, and have fun. Scott was my defender. Every time someone would try picking on me, he'd tell them to shut up, tell me to ignore them, and that what they'd say about me wasn't true.

My classmates sometimes would tease me and tell me,

"Jen's got a boyfriend."

I was so innocent, and naive that I'd say,

"I do."

Scott and I were inseparable friends. We'd leave the building together when school was over, and would play together all the time. When Scott would approach his father, he would start shouting,

"Dad, that's Jennifer! My best friend!" He'd repeat himself every five seconds.

"Okay, I've seen her. Now please shut up!" His father would reply.

On a rainy day, when all the students had to stay inside for recess, Scott and I had sat on the school floor and started working on a puzzle. For a moment, he stopped what he was doing and looked at me.

"Jennifer." Scott called out my name as he looked at me.

"What?" I asked as I stared at his brown eyes.

"Someday I want to marry you." He replied.

I smiled, and then innocently replied,

"I'm still too young but, I can when I get older."

"Okay." Scott answered.

"Oh, I want three kids. A boy, and two girls. Is that okay?" I asked all thrilled.

It seemed like I was planning my wedding, and future at such a young age!

However, what really mattered to me was that he saw me when I was invisible to others.

"Yeah, that's good." He had smiled.

When the school year was over, my mother was so happy that I had passed Kindergarten with flying colors. I had no trouble with my proceeding school years, and was an honor student. I loved school, and enjoyed learning and playing with my friends, especially Scotty.

On snow days when school would be cancelled I'd cry because, I wanted to go to school. School was like a second home for me, where I felt comfortable and could be my own little self.

When I had gained some confidence in myself, I started singing with my friends, and bringing a school audience at our feet at the school basement. My friends and I would stand on top of the school benches, and sing songs from the "New Kids on The Block." One of our favorite songs was "Hanging Tough." At the end of the song we'd twirl around, and jump off the benches. I had no shame, and thought I had all the fame. I loved to show off my spirit. Although, there were times when I was quite bossy.

"I think we should practice singing a bit more." I'd tell my friends.

"Why should we bother any way? Half of the school just makes fun and laughs at us." Crystal would tell me.

"Who cares about what they think? We are getting good." I'd reply.

I could have been a bit on the pushy side when things weren't my way but, over time I learned from my mistakes. I became a better person, and a popular student. Everyone ended up liking me because, I was sweet, and had a very pleasant personality.

I had friends at home too. Sometimes I would play with my cousin Melanie that lived on the second floor, and sometimes with Cristina and her older sister Silvia next door. Almost every Saturday, Cristina's mother would make pancakes for breakfast and have one of her daughters call me to have breakfast with them. Sometimes, I'd go to Cristina's house to play Barbie dolls. After playing, we would make some chocolate and marshmallow treats with gram crackers.

Almost every weekend, I'd take off to Cristina's house to play. We'd play Barbie dolls most of the time and spent hours playing.

One day while we were going to continue our little soap opera, I noticed that Silvia was ironing clothes for her mother. I didn't want her to feel left out and so I questioned,

"Silvia, do you want to play dolls with us?"

"No. I have to iron these clothes. I am a mature lady now. I can't be playing with dolls" Silvia replied.

She had just turned thirteen, and since she was a teenager now, she considered herself too old to play with Barbie dolls.

"Oh well. At least I asked." I thought as I smiled at her.

We continued our soap opera. I was a married woman with three children and Cristina was a married woman with four children, and we were in the middle of a family reunion.

My parents continued working hard to support one another, and I. They were both very happy to see me adapting well in school, and also with my next door friends and cousins. Everything seemed to be running smooth, and almost perfect but, it didn't last for long.

"Mrs. Wright!" My mother's manager shouted.

"What!" My mother asked in worry.

"Your daughter's principal is on the phone."

"Oh my God! What happened to my daughter?!" My mother said as she picked up the phone.

"Yes, Mr. Rhodes. What's wrong with my daughter?"

"Your daughter had a seizure, and fell down a flight of stairs."

"Oh my god! Is she ok?"

"She's ok but, severely bruised."

"I'm leaving work right now to pick her up!"

"Thank you, Mrs. Wright."

When my mother arrived at the principal's office, I was curled up in a corner crying.

"Are you okay, honey?" My mother knelt beside me.

"My legs and hands are hurting me, mommy." I wept.

"Mommy will put ice when we get home to make it feel better." She told me.

"Thanks for calling me, Mr. Rhodes." My mother told my principal.

"That's what we're here for. You're welcome!" My principal replied.

My mother brought me home, and rubbed ice on my legs as she started to cry.

"Torture will never end in our life! Will it?!" My mother said in despair.

After rubbing ice on my legs, my mother suggested me to take an evening nap. She draped a thin pink blanket over my legs, and handed me my teddy bear known as my "Friend."

"I love you, mommy." I whispered.

"I love you too, sweet cake." My mother smiled.

Later that night while I was still awoke, I heard my parents arguing in their bedroom.

"Andrew. Today I received a call from Jennifer's principal, and I had to pick her up from school because, she fell down a flight of stairs due to a seizure." My mother said.

"Maybe she was just tired, and lost her balance. I'm sure it's nothing to worry about." My father replied.

My father was a very optimistic individual. Sometimes too optimistic. He thought that because everything was going smooth in his life now, he wouldn't have to face any other obstacles. He wasn't a realistic individual, especially when trouble dawned in his family.

"Well, I think it is something to worry about." My mother argued.

"Our daughter is fine! You have to stop being so pessimistic. Have a little bit of faith!" My father answered.

"No! I think you have to stop being optimistic all the time, and face reality. If our daughter was tired, she wouldn't attempt to walk down those stairs! Ok? Our little girl wouldn't risk it!" My mother was furious.

"I'm still not convinced. It didn't work, honey." My father grinned.

"You jerk! This is our daughter we're talking about!"

With that remark I heard my mother jump out of bed.

"If this happens again, I myself will bring Jennifer to see a doctor! Got that?!" My mother was so mad.

"Ok. I'm sorry, honey. I just can't see our daughter getting sick again. That's all."

"You have to be a bit realistic too you know! Life won't always be filled with treasures." My mother replied.

"Come here. I'll cheer you up." My father replied.

"You're not joking with me. Are you?" My mother was serious.

"No! Not at all. I promise you that if Jennifer has another episode, we'll take her to see a doctor. Now will you come here?" My father asked in despair.

"I'd love to!" My mother laughed.

I hated when they argued because, it would make me sad. I liked to see those two lovebirds happy and united.

After that first episode in school, I started having many episodes. One day my mother had left me with my grandmother and while I was playing, all of a sudden I started shaking with tremors and couldn't see. I called out for my grandmother as I slurred my speech.

"Grandma. I'm cold, and I can't see. I can only see black, and I feel very tired." After that remark, I passed out.

My grandmother was in panic, and called Children's hospital where I was being followed up with my Plastic Surgeon. I had faced another seizure, and it seemed like every time I faced one, it would get worse and worse on me.

I was admitted to Children's Hospital by ambulance, and my grandmother accompanied me. While a doctor examined me, my grandmother called my mother at work.

"Miranda!" My grandmother shouted in frenzy.

"What! What's wrong?!" My mother shouted back.

"Jennifer had another terrible seizure, and I had to call Children's Hospital. They picked her up by ambulance, and a doctor is examining her right now."

"Oh, dear Lord!" My mother cried.

"I'll be there as soon as I possibly can." My mother replied as she tasted her tears that touched her lips as she talked, and cried at the same time.

After a two-hour drive, my mother finally arrived at the hospital.

"Where is she?!" My mother asked in panic.

"They transferred her to a room because, they want her to stay overnight." My grandmother replied.

"What?! Why?!"

"They want to perform studies on her."

"Oh, no! My daughter is no science project! I want to speak with the doctor this instant!" My mother was furious.

When my mother finally had a chance to meet with the doctor that had examined me, she asked,

"Why are you keeping my daughter?"

"We just want to see what kind of medication is best for her." The doctor replied.

"What medication? You mean to tell me that my little girl will have to take medication for the rest of her life?!"

"No. Not at all. It will only be for a short period of time." The doctor replied.

"Look here! Do what you need to do but, please don't use my daughter as one of your science projects. She's my little girl, and she's been through enough."

"Not a problem, Mrs. Wright. I will take good care of your daughter and as a matter of fact, if you'd like to stay with her I can arrange for that."

"I'd appreciate that." My mother calmed herself down.

After speaking with the doctor, my mother called my father. My father was home sleeping from a hard night at work.

"Hello?" My father answered the phone half asleep.

"Honey. It's Miranda."

"Hey, honey. What's going on?" My father asked.

"I'm at Children's hospital with Jennifer. She had a terrible seizure at my mother's house this morning, and is staying overnight at the hospital."

"What?" My father asked as he finally came to his senses.

"Is she ok?" He asked.

"Yeah. I'm going to stay with her so she won't be afraid."

"Is she coming home tomorrow?" My father asked.

"She should be. I hope." My mother replied.

"Give her a hug and kiss for me." My father told my mother.

"I will. I'm going to miss you." My mother smiled.

"I'm going to miss you too." My father replied as he kissed the phone.

"It seems like every night you have off, something goes wrong." My mother was frustrated.

"That's the way life is, darling." He replied.

"Darling? You never called me darling before. I like that."

"I love you, Miranda." My father whispered.

"I love you too, darling." My mother laughed.

The following day I went home, and on our way home, my mother stopped at the pharmacy to pick up my medication.

As time moved on, I became seizure free. It had been three months now that I was seizure free, and my doctor gave my parents the authority to stop my medication to see if I'd prove to be seizure free without it. Indeed, I was seizure free without the medication, and this made my doctor and my parents very happy.

When I turned seven, my parents decided to talk with my Plastic Surgeon about reconstructing the left of my face. Dr. Holmes was delighted with the approach of constructive plastic surgery, and assured my parents that I would benefit from it.

My doctor had one of his secretaries schedule an appointment for an evaluation on me, and also had his secretary call his team of surgeons that he worked with to participate with their ideas on my case. Each surgeon had found some time to look through my portfolio, and study my case. They were stunned when they viewed my pictures. They had seen plenty of Hemangiomas but, nothing like mine. The first thing that came to their minds was the question of where they'd begin?

3

Life Goes on

When my parents and I arrived at the doctors office, we walked into a room where there were families that had sons and daughters with the same condition I had. However, mine was much larger. It seemed like Hemangiomas were popular but yet, there were no drugs or medications to completely stop the growth of this terrifying blood tumor. Prednisone would only prolong its growth until the Hemangioma reached its quiescent stage. The tumor its self had a mind of it's own, and stopped when it was fully satisfied.

"Mommy, they look like me." I said with such sorrow.

"Yeah. I know, honey. They're going to look beautiful just like you." My mother told me as she slid her hand down my long light brown hair.

"Jennifer Wright." The nurse called.

"That's me." I replied as I got up from my seat, and stood on my tippy toes smiling.

"Hi there! Are these your parents?" The nurse asked me.

"Yeah. This is my mom, and this is my dad." I replied.

"I'm pleased to meet both of you. Now if you'd please follow me."

The nurse took my parents and I down a long corridor where there were many doors on both sides with doctors' names engraved on wooden plaques.

"Mommy, I want to be a doctor someday." I proudly replied as I followed the nurse.

"You do?!" My mother was delighted with the idea.

"Yeah. I want to help people like me." I replied.

"You'll make a fine doctor, sweetie!" The nurse smiled at me.

"Thanks." I replied.

"The doctor will be in shortly with some co-workers of his. Is that all right?" The nurse asked.

"Of course! The more doctors, the better!" My father replied.

My doctor came in, and his team of surgeons.

"Hi, Miss Jennifer!" The doctor said.

"Hi." I replied as I tried hiding my shyness.

"Oh, and this is the famous Mr. and Mrs. Wright." My doctor proudly told his co-workers.

"Jennifer, these are some of my friends who are here to help me make smart decisions on making you look like a beautiful princess."

"Like Cinderella?" My eyes widened.

"Certainly!" My doctor laughed.

His team of surgeons smiled and replied,

"Much prettier!"

"Ok. Now where do we start?" My doctor asked his surgeons.

"She has a lot of stretched skin. Maybe we can take off some extra skin, and lift her left eyelid a bit." One of his surgeons replied.

"That's a good start. Is there anything else any of you would like to add?" Dr. Holmes asked.

"Her upper lip. We can take off excess tissue, and form her lip as best as we can." Another surgeon replied.

"Her nose. Maybe we can take off some excess tissue there too, and try to shape her nose." Another surgeon replied.

"Looks like we have a plan here. I'm impressed. Mr. and Mrs. Wright. Are you grasping the concept of this?"

"Yes we are, and we know that we can trust you and your co-workers Dr. Holmes." My mother smiled.

Before we left the doctor's office, one of my doctor's secretaries booked my first constructive plastic surgery.

When that day arrived, my mother gathered some things to bring with her since she was going to stay with me overnight at the hospital after surgery. When we arrived at the operating room, I was given a Johnny and some hospital slippers.

"Have her take everything off from the waist up, Mrs. Wright." The nurse told my mother.

"Mommy, is it going to hurt?" I asked as I lie down on the hospital bed with my favorite teddy bear known as my "Friend."

"No, honey. You'll be asleep." My mother replied.

After a while, the nurse came back and asked me what fruit flavor I liked best.

"I like orange." I told her.

Since I was only seven years of age, my doctor didn't want to traumatize me with an intravenous line. Instead of an intravenous line, they had special masks made for children undergoing surgery. These masks were made for children to breathe in sleeping medication. The medication came in different fruit flavors to make breathing comfortable, and desirable.

At approximately half an hour after I was given the mask, I was sound asleep from the anesthetics. As one of the nurses wheeled my bed into the surgery room, my mother started crying. My father was a strong lad, and had always kept the pain to himself. However, today he couldn't hold back his emotions. His eyes became red, and stung from him forcing himself to hold the tears back.

Four hours later, I was placed in the recovery room.

"She did very well." The nurse whispered to my parents, while I was still sound asleep.

When I woke up, I was happy to see my parents by my side. My mother came up to me, gave me a kiss, and gave me a gift for being so brave. It was a real stethoscope.

"You'll need this when you become a doctor." My mother smiled at me.

"Thank you, mommy! Now I can listen to my heart." I replied.

A few minutes later, I wasn't feeling so good. "Mommy! I don't feel so good. I feel like I need to throw up."

"Hold on. Mommy's going to call a nurse."

The nurse gave me a bassinet to vomit in, and also gave me nausea medication. I vomited blood, and whatever I had left in my stomach.

"This is normal, Mrs. Wright. Anesthetics usually cause nausea, and the blood is from the surgery." The nurse explained.

The following day I was discharged, and my mother threw a little party at home for me.

Everyone in my family called me the brave princess.

The following week, I went back to the doctor's office to remove stitches.

My parents were worried because, they knew it was going to hurt.

"Jennifer. I'm going to take out your stitches. It's going to hurt a little bit but, if you are a brave girl, I'll give you lots of pretty stickers." The doctor told me.

"Ok." I smiled.

As my doctor pulled out the stitches, I cried and tried my very best to be brave. After he finished, I wiped my tears, and then asked,

"Was I brave?"

"Yes, you were." The doctor replied.

"Can I have some stickers?" I asked.

"Of course! Mrs. Dunkin, could you please show Jennifer where our sticker bin is?"

"Most certainly! Come this way, little one." The secretary replied.

I picked out a handful of stickers, and was so happy. The smallest things in life would make me so happy. I wasn't greedy but instead, appreciated what I had and made the best of it.

Every year on my summer vacation, I would have another constructive surgery done. Doctors were making progress, my parents were pleased with their hard work, and so was I. My image improved every year, and it seemed like every year I became more comfortable with my appearance.

Time had passed by, and my mother was now eight months pregnant with another child. It had been nine years before my parents decided in having another child mostly because, I was a very sick child, and needed a lot of love and attention.

I was so excited that soon I would have a baby sister or brother to play with. Most of the time I wasn't lonely because, I would play with my friends next door and my cousins but when they weren't home, I'd feel lonely at times.

My mother wasn't very fond about going to mass. She was like many people who say they're Catholic, and don't bother going to mass. She believed that those who pray at home and are faithful to the Lord, are better heard than those who attend mass just to say they were there.

"Yeah. He or she was there all right, sleeping through the entire gospel." My mother would always say.

Despite my mother's opinion about attending mass, when she was pregnant she felt the need to participate. Every week she'd make a sacrifice to attend mass, and in every mass she'd cry and ask,

"Oh, dear God! Please bring a healthy child into this world. We wouldn't be able to bear the pain of having another sick child. Please have mercy on us!"

My parents were very happy about having another child but, beneath this happiness there were also worry and concern. There weren't really much they could do for it, except trusting in God.

They hadn't picked names yet because, they were stressing themselves out worrying about having another sick child.

"You know what?" My father told my mother.

"What?" My mother asked.

"Let's just leave it all in God's hands, and not worry about it anymore. What do you think?"

"I think you're right." My mother smiled.

"So, honey. Have you picked names?" My father asked.

"No. Not really. Although, yesterday at the bank there was this beautiful little girl looking out the window, and I asked her what her name was. She told me her name was Monique, and also told me that she was a pro at making snow angels as she looked at the snow outside the window."

"That's a pretty name. What if it's a boy?" My father asked as he smiled.

"If it's a boy, we can call him Andrew Jr." My mother laughed.

"I know you like my name but, do you really want another Andrew in the house? Then later on, an Andrew the third?" My father laughed.

"Don't get smart. Fine. You decide." My mother laughed.

"What about, John?" My father asked.

"John?" My mother thought.

"Yeah! Jennifer and John make a good ring tone. Don't you think?" My father asked. "Jennifer and John! Come here! Yeah, I guess so!" My mother laughed.

All of my parents' friends, and family were confident it was going to be a boy.

"Your face didn't change much. It's definitely going to be a boy." One of my mother's friends would tell her.

I thought differently. I was almost certain my mother was going to have a baby girl because, I had a dream of going to the library with my sister. It was a dream of the future. Could I be right?

"Mommy. I'm going to have a baby sister! I know because, I had a dream!" I'd tell my mother.

"Oh, yeah?" My mother would laugh.

The weeks seemed to fly by, and my mother's due date was only two weeks away. As my mother woke up, she headed for the bathroom to prompt herself for work. As she curled her hair, she took a quick glance at the calender and said,

"Gosh, I can't believe it's already December 19. Just two more weeks, and this baby will be sprung!" My mother laughed.

She had then gone to work, but didn't end up making it through the entire day. My father had to pick her up and bring her to the hospital because, her water broke.

At seven in the evening, my mother gave birth to another baby girl. I was right! See that! Sometimes I feel as if I have a sixth sense because, sometimes I can feel when something is bound to happen or is happening. It's strange but, so there. I call it my "Deja Vu." As my mother held her newborn for the first time, she cradled my sister and then looked at my father who was standing beside her with a smile that reached from cheek to cheek.

"It's a healthy baby girl." My mother happily replied.

"She's our little Monique Wright!" My father proudly replied.

"Would you like to hold her, honey?"

"Of course." My father extended his hardworking arms.

I then came in with my grandmother, and with a little stuffed animal I bought at the gift shop for my new sister. My parents were happy to see me, and asked me if I wanted to hold my baby sister.

"Yeah, mommy!" I replied in excitement.

"Be careful with her head, sweetie." My mother warned me.

The following day my parents brought my sister home. I was a big sister now, and was mommy's little helper. I was in charge of taking care of her while my mother went to work. My father was always home but sleeping from long work nights, and so, I was the one with the babysitting duties. I would feed her, change her diapers, play with her, and would always try to keep her quiet so my father could sleep. I loved making my baby sister laugh with some puppets I would make out of old socks. I was very happy with my sister. However, I was quite upset that my privilege of playing with my friends, and cousins were cut. Sometimes, I felt as if I were older than what I really was.

In addition, this wasn't the only thing I was upset about. I was also upset about not being the center of attention to the family anymore. Before my sister was born, my grandparents, aunts, and uncles would spoil and baby me to death. I loved being with my aunt Nancy. She was still single, and had all the time in the world to play with me. Many times I would go up to her room, and would dance with this big doll that was my height to the song, "I'll be home with bells on" from Dolly Parton. When Christmas came around, I'd bug my aunt Nancy to bring me Christmas shopping. I had my own savings account, and every Christmas I'd have my mother take some money out so I could buy Christmas presents for my parents, and sister.

I had been the family's great focus for nine years, and I just couldn't adapt to the sudden change. Jealousy crept up into my little heart. It took a while before I could understand that I was a big girl now, and should know that my family loves me without them showing it.

Four years had gone by so quickly, and I had completed my sixth constructive surgery at the age of thirteen. My image had improved drastically, and my doctor was amazed with his and his team's work.

My doctor told us that he wanted to wait until I stopped growing before performing another surgery. My parents approved. They thought that it was a good idea because, this was sort of being a routine for me of going to the operating room, and then pulling out stitches every summer. It was time for me to get a break, and a summer vacation to enjoy.

My parents worked hard to make up for the extra family member, and they were very happy. Things seemed to be just right, and perfect until something comes into their life that almost destroys their marriage, and their feelings for each other. That something was a parish. A different religion.

4

Saving a Marriage

"Hey, honey! You know when you tell me that mass is boring?" My father asked.

"Yeah. What about it?" My mother asked.

"I saw this commercial on T.V. about this Christian church in New Bedford. They make preaching fun. They dance, and sing praising the Lord. Some people claim that God made a miracle in their life since they've attended that church."

"Are you serious?" My mother asked in astonishment.

"Of course, I'm serious! I think we should try it. What do you think?" My father asked.

"We can give it a try." My mother agreed.

The parish had sessions every day, and my parents would go Monday thru Friday at seven o'clock every week. They seemed to like it very much. I would take care of my sister while they were at mass, and would be grateful when my sister would fall asleep while watching the "Banana Split Show." Sometimes they'd take me too but, I always had to watch my sister in the back with the other kids and never had a chance to listen to what they preached.

In this new parish, my parents were taught a different way to approach God. The pastors taught you how to speak to the Lord like a friend, with respect and love. They believed that confession should only be done with God and no one else, and that one should pray to God and not the saints because, God is the only savior.

After two months in this parish, my father started slipping away because he noticed something wasn't right. He was noticing that the pastors were more interested in what their people could offer, than seeing them get closer to God.

"Who is going to make a sacrifice of a hundred dollars? Raise your hand." The pastor would shout on the microphone.

"God is watching you, and is seeing that you're making a sacrifice for him." The pastor would say.

They used God, in order to make people pour out their money. They didn't care if one was poor, and couldn't give much. They were just greedy for the money. Majority of the parishioners were blinded by this scam, and truly believed that if one gave all they had, God would reward them at the end. My mother was also blinded by this scam, and didn't want to believe my father. Every day there would be a fight at home, and my sister and I would end up crying. It seemed like our sweet life had turned into one big nightmare.

"Miranda, I've told you so many times! They just want to suck up our money! It's all a bunch of bullshit! They don't care about God. They just care about the money! Money! It's all about money!" My father tried holding his temper.

"No. It's not all about money! I feel God's presence there! What?! You're going to deny that too." My mother replied with such vicious eyes.

"No, honey. I'm not saying that. You can pray the same way at home, and you'll still feel the presence of God. Don't you get what I'm saying?" My father asked.

"I don't care what you say! I'm going, and you can't stop me!" My mother replied.

"You know what? I don't need or deserve this. I don't even know you anymore. I'm packing my bags this instant, and I'm out of here!" My father was heartbroken.

"No! Andrew please don't leave! I love you!" My mother cried as she fell to her kneels in front of him.

"You don't love me! You love them!" My father replied in disgrace, and then walked by her with a cold heart that had been stabbed by the woman he loved.

My father walked out the door as soon as he finished packing. My mother was crying, and screaming at the same time as she lie on the floor all soaked with her tears.

"Oh, my God! What did I do?! What did I do?!" My mother mourned.

I was terrified. I never thought this could've happened to us. They were always so united and bonded that I could've never imagined that something would break the strong bond they had for each other. I cried against my pillow, and covered my ears because, it hurt me to hear them say those horrible things to each other.

About half an hour later, my father comes back.

"Andrew! Darling! You came back! I love you so much, honey!" My mother wept as she wrapped her arms around my father.

"Get your hands off of me!" My father replied.

My mother brought her arms down, and stared at him with teary eyes.

"I came back for the kids! Not for you!" I could see the hurt in my father's eyes. He had a bleeding heart that lost its touch. Deep down inside he was dying to forgive and love her again but, he was just too hurt. That night they slept in separate rooms. That was one of the saddest days of my life.

As time moved on, my parents started getting along. My father would ignore the fact that my mother still went to that parish because, he truly loved her and didn't want to lose her.

"Honey. We have enough money in the bank, and I think it's a good time to move to the Azores. We will build our dream house, and live a wonderful life out there! You won't have to work because

I'll be selling fish, and will make enough money for us to live off of. What do you say?" My father asked.

My mother didn't want to move to the Azores because, she didn't know anyone out there except for a few cousins, and my father's family. She knew that she was on thin ice with my father, and knew that saying yes would make him very happy.

"This is a way to bring our marriage back to life like it was before." My mother thought.

"I'd love to!" My mother replied.

Change wasn't all that easy, especially for my mother. My father on the other hand, was satisfied with his decision and was determined to start a new life in the Azores. He always had this illusion, and obsession that the Azores were a better place where there would be more abundance, and better quality of living. He was so blinded by his family who had moved out there before him. They would tell him that the Azores were the true America where there were no stress, and plenty of entertainment.

I was now fourteen years of age. I could have been a teen but, I still wasn't grasping the gravity of this situation. It only hit me when I finally saw the big trailer truck outside getting filled up with our furniture, and possessions. As I stared out the window, my eyes grew heavy as I tried holding the tears back. I knew now that this was it, and that this was the last time I would probably see my family and friends.

Before our departure, my grandmother, my mother's mother, compassionately hugged my mother as she felt the soreness of her throat while she cried and cried. When she turned around to hug me and my sister, her cries grew stronger.

"I'm going to miss you girls so much!" My grandmother cried.

My mother's father, my grandfather, being a strong lad that he was, also cried. My grandparents then gave my father a hand shake, a hug, and wished him a good flight. They liked my father. There was no mistake about that but, they were a bit upset that he was taking their daughter, and granddaughters away from them. My mother wanted to reveal her true emotions but, she kept them to herself because she was afraid my father may not like it. She felt trapped, and hated knowing that she was abandoning her family and friends as she still agreed to move.

She could have put her foot down right there in the airport in front of her parents. She could have told my father she wasn't leaving her homeland and her family but, she didn't. Instead she sacrificed everything she had, and went somewhere where she had nothing and no one just to make her husband happy. She truly loved him. Not every woman would sacrifice so much for their spouse but, she did.

My mother would always bend down to keep peace in her marriage, and family. Fighting with my father was like ripping her heart out of her chest. She knew that no marriage would be perfect. Besides, my father was a good husband. It's true he had some issues when decisions had to be made among the family but, in reality he was a respectful, and decent spouse and father.

The Azores were a group of nine islands, and Terceira was one of the nine islands where my father and his family were brought up. My father was determined to start a new life there. He kept augmenting to my mother's expectations of having a life anyone could dream of. However, he wasn't even sure that what he was saying would be true.

We moved into my father's eldest sister's house where my father's parents were living. His eldest sister was the only one still in America because, her daughters hadn't adapted to the change of lifestyles when they initially moved to the Azores. My parents were only living there until they could find their own private place while the building of their dream house was being constructed. They liked their own privacy, and besides my father's mother, my grandmother, would drive them crazy sometimes. She would baby them so much, and they would get so sick of it. They felt like they were teens again.

"Andrew. Honey. Where are you both going?" My grandmother would ask.

"Mom. We're going to the city." My father would sigh.

"Oh, but what time will you be home?" She'd question him.

"We don't know. We'll get home when we get home." My father would reply abruptly.

"Oh, dear! Both of you can't go to the city dressed like that!" She'd tell them.

My parents were well dressed in jeans, and nice T-shirts but, that wasn't enough to impress my grandmother. She expected my mother to be wearing a nice dress, and my father to be wearing a suit wherever they went.

"We look fine!" My father would tell her as we'd take off.

My paternal grandmother was a fine lady, and very proper. My father was her only live son. She had two sons before my father but, they didn't survive. They died at such a young age, and this was one of the reasons why she babied him so much. Above all, she was a very caring and sweet person who wanted the best for her children and family. A mother will always be a mother, and a mother will always worry over the tiniest things that relate to their loved ones. No one or nothing will ever be able change that, and some worry more than others. That's just that way life is.

After about a month, we moved to one of my father's friend's house. George, my father's friend rented his house to my parents since him and his wife where still living in America. It was a quiet neighborhood, and on the left side of the house there was a small beach close by. My parents were so glad that privacy, and comfort were a part of their life again.

A few days later, our furniture arrived from overseas, and everything was intact. Now that we were finally settled, we were ready to begin a new life.

Early the next morning we woke up with the sound of the next door neighbor's rooster screeching "Cock-a-doodle-do." That same day, we went to register me in school. I didn't speak the language very well, and couldn't read or write. Many neighbors had told my mother that I might need to start school all over again. I in no particular way wanted start over again, and so the school gave me a chance by placing me in 8th grade where I belonged.

"Have her give it a try, Mrs. Wright. You just never know. She may even be one of the smartest in her class someday." The school director told my mother.

"My daughter is very intelligent, and I think she will do just fine." My mother replied.

"I'd also like to inform you that class material here is much harder than what students expect in America. The course material is equivalent to American college levels. I hope that won't be a downfall for her." The school director told my mother.

"She'll try, Mrs. De Oliveira. My daughter is a bright student. You'll be surprised." My mother replied.

Although my mother applauded me, deep down inside she wasn't so sure about me being able to defeat this challenge. She had many doubts.

"Well then. I wish her the best of luck." The director replied.

I was somewhat happy about starting school again but, was afraid and nervous about attending a new school. I was mostly afraid that students may make fun of me like they used to when I was a child. I kept asking myself the same questions.

"Will they like me? Will I make any friends?" I worried.

Although my image had improved drastically, I was still subconscious of myself. As I approached my teen years, it grew worse and worse for me. I had very little to no self-esteem, and self-confidence. I only felt safe when I was with friends or family. I was always afraid people, especially guys would just stare and walk away like some did when I was a child. I knew that the first thing that attracted men were the looks most of the time, and I was afraid that no guy would ever bother approaching me. It hurt me to think this way but, this was how I felt. To me I was a beautiful person inside but, not so beautiful outside. I knew that very few men looked at a girl's insides before looking at a girl's outsides, and this bothered me so much.

"Why couldn't I have been born beautiful like every other girl?" I'd ask myself as I looked in the mirror.

"I'm so ugly, and will never find a date. Guys won't even care to look at me because, my defect destroys all my beauty." I'd cry.

That night before my first day of school, I couldn't sleep. I kept tossing and turning with the thought of how my first day would turn out to be. In the morning I felt incredibly sloth wrapped in my thick blankets, and didn't feel like getting up. I was nervous. I was very nervous about starting all over again.

I had no clue what I was going to wear, but made an attempt to look in my closet. There I spotted this flowered dress.

"I think this will do." I told myself.

After getting ready, I headed for the bus stop. As I entered the city bus, I felt my whole body shake. I was so nervous, and it felt so hard for me to keep my cool. After I got off the bus, I felt somewhat relieved. Relieved that no bully had called me names, or threw an eraser at me.

I ended up making many friends at my new school. Everyone wanted to be around me and get to know me because, I was an American. They were all surprised to see that I considered myself no better than they were. My friends would call the American's snobs because, those who lived there would always put their nose up in the air, and think they were better than the Portugese population but, they couldn't call me a snob. I wasn't a snob at all. I was simple, friendly, and sweet they'd say.

My friends were the ones who made me like school, even though I wasn't doing well in my classes due to my language difficulties. However, perfect can never exist in my life. When things ran smooth, it never lasted that way. Not for long. Anyway.

I started getting picked on by a couple of guys because of my glasses. Students in Terceira wore the small oval European style. My glasses were big and round like a circles. They sort of looked like satellite dishes, and this was exactly what they'd call them.

I didn't let this get to me. In one way I was relieved because, they were picking on something that could be corrected, unlike my defect that could only be corrected up to a certain point.

Out of the blue during class recess, this guy named Luis had the courage to approach me while I was with my friends. He thought he was going to win, but he was so wrong.

"Hey, you with the satellite dishes." Luis chuckled.

I turned around and as I looked him in the eye with a smirk on my face, I knew exactly what I was going to say.

"Well. You don't look so hot either! Pizza face!" I replied.

"I can't believe you said that. You stuck up for yourself. You go girl!" My friends started laughing hysterically.

Luis turned all different shades of red as he walked away. After that day he never picked on me again. I guess he hated his acne, and me telling him off made him feel worse.

I had learned to be a tough person. I had to be. I wasn't going to let anyone else bring me down. I had plenty of that when I was a child. All I wanted now was happiness. I wanted to laugh and have fun with my friends, and wanted to be no different from anyone else. I wanted to succeed in learning the Portuguese language, and move on along with my friends.

I was always a very happy person who loved to socialize with, and help others. There wasn't much that would bring me down mostly because I had suffered so much and to me, there weren't many things that would hurt me beyond what I've already faced. Besides, I ended up being loved by everyone who knew me, and all the new friends I made along the way. My friends always had something good to say about me when they talked about me. I had shared my happy, live, and loving spirit with everyone whether they were rich or poor. What mattered to me was a person's insides.

Although I was happy with the friends I made, my classes weren't going so well. I could read very little, and couldn't write. This turned out to be a great problem, and a great challenge for me. The first two semesters were very tough. I failed test after test. Sometimes I would come home crying.

"I can't do this, mom. I just can't!" I'd tell her in despair.

My mother never knew what to say. She knew it was as hard on me as it was for her. My mother couldn't find a job because, she had the same difficulties I had. She couldn't even write out a check.

My father had no job either. He had told my mother he was going to sell fish. He had gone for his physical and licenses. He was all prepared. Then after all of that, he decides to change his mind.

"I want a real job, Miranda. I don't want to be coming home smelling like fish every day." My father told my mother.

"Oh, now you tell me that?" My mother questioned him.

"Sorry, honey. Watch. I'll find a job very soon. I promise."

"You promise this and that! It's easy for you to say. You promised me a better life out here, and so far I haven't seen it. Better for you because, this is your homeland where you have all your family and friends but, not better for me and our daughter who struggle to understand the language. Besides, I don't have anyone out here. I feel so lonely, and so isolated. Can't you see?" My mother argued.

"Don't worry, honey. You'll make friends once you find a job."
My father replied.

"A Job? How am I going to find a job if I can't read and write the
language? You don't bother thinking about all the facts. You think
every thing is just meant to fall in our hands but, that's not how life
works. I don't have the qualifications for any job here." My mother
replied.

My father was puzzled. He didn't know what to say. He knew
my mother was right, and almost felt like he had made a big mistake
in bringing us out here. My mother was getting frustrated, and I was
always coming home depressed with poor test grades.

For a while my father pondered on the thought of moving back
to America but, a job as a security guard came up. This made my
father very happy, and he tried to make us happy too. Many times
we'd have picnics at Mount Brasil, and my father also made an
effort to find my mother's three cousins. They were three brothers,
and their names were Leonel, Seraphim, and Luis. This made my
mother very happy. At least now she had some family. Sometimes
Leonel would have cook outs, and would invite us over. My sister
and I loved picking grapes from his vineyard. He had a big vineyard
and when it was grape season, he'd always invite us to help him pick
grapes to make wine.

Things were finally falling in to play. Our house was being constructed, and there was money coming in. I was doing better in
school sacrificing myself to double study. I'd try to understand what
I was studying first. Then I'd really study once I knew what majority
of the material I was studying meant, and how to write understand-
able statements about the material. I was one hard worker, and
learned the language all by myself with no tutor or any special support. I'd study for hours and hours, exhausting my brain cells. Most
of the effort I put in was because, I loved being with my friends.
They were the one's who had motivated me to defeat the challenge

and make it work. My friends also helped me a lot. Sometimes I'd borrow their notebooks to read, and compare their notes to mine. My cousin Monica would also help me with my homework, and would make sure I understood the material.

Winters in the Azores were very different from the ones in Massachusetts. They were very windy, rainy and very damp. When I mean windy, I mean close to hurricane winds. There was no snow which was a blessing but, when it rained it poured.

On a winter day at five in the morning, all were sound sleep except for my mother. As she looked out the bedroom window, she heard the whistle of wind that was seeping beneath the window and window sill. Electric and phone wires swung back and forth, and tree branches were being blown in the same direction as the wind.

My mother was afraid of sending me to school in this weather because it was like hurricane weather, and so she decided to keep me home from school.

"Jennifer. Wake up!" My mother called me.

"What mom? It's still early. It's only five thirty." I told my mother half asleep.

"You're staying home today because, it's lousy out there. It's like a hurricane out there." My mother told me.

"But mom, I can't have that many absences." I was worried.

"It's only for one day. Besides, your teachers will understand." My mother replied.

My mother thought they would understand but, they didn't. When I went to school the following day, my teacher had asked me why I was absent.

"My mother didn't want me going out in hurricane weather." I replied.

"This is not hurricane weather! Is your mother insane?! We have this kind of weather all season long. Both of you are just in need of a little getting used to. That's all." The teacher replied.

"Mrs. Medeiros. You have to be a bit more understanding. Jennifer, and her family are not used to this kind of weather. They're used to the snow." George stood up for me.

After George's little speech, the teacher gave no response. Not just George but everyone in my class was proud to have an American in their class, and most of all for me being a decent American. When English class would be in session, all my classmates would hover around me for answers. I felt bad for one boy in particular who was failing English along with some other courses. In addition, this was his third time repeating 8th grade. His name was Mario. He was tall, built, and had short black hair.

The only subject I was good at was English, and this was the only subject I could help him with.

"I what to go to the cinema means, Eu quero ir para o cinema." I would explain to him. "Cinema! I know that word!" Mario happily told me in Portugese.

"Waannt to goo to the cinema wit me?" Mario could barely pronounce the words.

"I'll think about it." I told him in Portugese with a smile that reached from cheek to cheek.

I never brought up that issue of going to the cinema again, and neither did he. It's not that I didn't want to go out with him but because, I barely knew him. I felt like I needed some time to get to know him, and be able to trust him. This was the first time someone had ever asked me out. Besides, I didn't know where to begin. On the other hand, he seemed to be interested in me because if he didn't, he wouldn't have asked me out.

Mario was a very sweet person. He loved to joke around, and loved to smile and laugh. I started helping him constantly with his English homework, and it seemed like every time I helped him, I felt like he was getting more and more attracted to me. Every time we worked on an assignment he'd get closer and closer to me. At times I'd get so nervous, and turn shades of red. This was the first time a guy had approached me that way, and inside I was so delighted to know that he was the first to look at my insides before anything else.

Sometimes I'd crank the perfume before I'd go to school, and when he'd come and sit beside me he'd sniff me and tell me I smelt beautiful. I'd smile and he'd smile too. We'd joke and play around together. Sometimes he'd stick leaves on my hair while I'd be talking to my friends, or pull my hair and hide so I wouldn't know who it was.

After a while he came up with the idea of playing around pretending to be boyfriend and girlfriend. He was so funny but yet, I wonder why he just wanted to pretend. He seemed to like me very much. Why didn't he want me to be his true girlfriend? We got along so well, and I liked him a lot too. The only thing that crossed my mind was that maybe he thought I deserved better? However, I didn't. He had everything I wanted, and most of all he appreciated me for whom I was, which was very important to me.

"Jennifer, I'm a loser. I can't even pass 8th grade." He'd tell me sometimes.

I'd get mad at him and tell him that he wasn't a loser, and that he just wasn't fit for school. Mario made me feel special, and wanted. He made me happy, and made me laugh. He loved to see my reaction when he mentioned about us being boyfriend and girlfriend. I'd get all red and shy. However, I knew he was just playing around and not serious.

One day in English class, we had to come up with a speech about tourism. Unfortunately, Mario wasn't in my group. He pretended to look devastated. It was so hilarious. A few minutes later, I hear him call out my name.

"Jenny!" He shouted.

I looked up, and saw him holding up a piece of his notebook paper. "I LOVE YOU" was written on the paper that he was waving back and forth. My face started getting beat red, and my heart sunk as he blew me a kiss. All our classmates were just staring at both of us, and this made me even redder. I felt like hiding under a desk.

After a while, Mario started putting his arm around me while we sat in class. The first time he wrapped his arm around me, I felt very nervous, and my body kept trembling. This was the first time that a guy had ever hugged me in such a special way. It felt so exciting. My face was bright red, and our teacher was just staring at me as if she were asking,

"Jennifer, what's wrong?"

One time in art class Mario and I were working on a project. Then all of a sudden Mario stops what he is doing, and keeps staring at me.

"What?" I started blushing.

"You have such beautiful eyes." He replied.

"Hey everyone! Come and look at Jennifer's eyes! Aren't they beautiful?" He announced to the entire class.

Two seconds ago I only had Mario's eyes staring at mine but now I had a million eyes staring at mine, and I became bashful.

February 14 had come quicker than ever. This was my first Valentine's here in the Azores, and I took it like any ordinary day because, I had no Valentine. I thought I didn't.

On our second class period, an elected student arrived at our classroom with all of the love letters to be delivered. As he called out the names, my name kept coming up, and I was totally shocked. I was the one who had received the most love letters in the class.

"Go, Jenny!" My friend Anna shouted.

I received seven love letters. Four were from Mario, and three were from another guy named Alonso from another 8th grade class.

"Whose are those other letters from? I only sent you four." Mario asked.

"They're from another guy from the class next door." I replied.

"Who? I want to know who he is because, I want to tell him to stay away from you. You're my girl." Mario pretended to be jealous.

"Let me see what he wrote you." Mario took one of the letters and read it. It said,

"Jennifer, I think you are a beautiful girl, and I love when you wear pink."

I really didn't think this guy liked me that way. I think he was playing around with me, and was set up by his friends who talked him into writing me a letter. Unfortunately, I was wearing pink that day and Mario noticed that.

"You're wearing pink! So, I guess you do like him." Mario was pretending to be mad and upset.

I knew he was just playing around but, I still liked to give him my sweet touch.

"I don't like him that way, Mario. I'm telling you the truth. Here, I brought some Valentine's chocolates just for you. Maybe this will cheer you up."

He smiled as he grabbed one. Then after eating it, he would go back to his upset mood. "Want another chocolate to cheer you up?" I asked.

He then took another one and devoured that one as well.

"Want another one?" I asked again.

"No. Thanks." He replied as he gave me a hug.

Mario once told me that I had a gift. He told me that I had a gift in making people happy. He always had something good to say about me, and it seemed to me that I was important to him.

On an easy school day when two teachers were absent and we only had one class session, Mario and I worked on our homework together. Then when it was time for our class, we went to the classroom and waited along with our other classmates. While we waited for the teacher to arrive, Mario and I were talking. Then all of a sudden when I was really close to him, he tells me,

"Jennifer, if you want to be my girlfriend, you've got to see what's down below." Mario smiled as he started to unbuckle his cowboy belt.

"Oh my God! I can't be seeing what I'm seeing! My virgin eyes!" I thought as he unbuckled his belt.

"Hey, man. Don't do that to the girl. You're going to traumatize the poor girl. Lighten up, man. Can't you see she's going to burst in flames?! Look at her! She looks like a tomato!" George replied.

After Mario looked at me and saw that I was all fevered, he stopped.

"You don't think I'd really do that to you. Huh?" Mario smiled.

"No but, I have to admit that for a moment I thought you were." I smiled back.

He laughed at my response. I loved to see him smile and laugh because, it made me smile and laugh too.

The school year had come to an end quicker than ever, and I was happy because I had passed 8th grade. It was borderline passing but considering that I was an American and didn't know the language very well, I made a great achievement. Mario didn't pass. I felt bad for him and felt sad that I was never going to see him again because, he was going to drop out. Yet. I wonder. If he did pass, would our friendship turn out to be something serious? He seemed to be very interested in me, and I myself liked him a lot too. Playing around was what had bonded us together. He always found a way to make me laugh and smile. I was going miss him, that's for sure. All I knew was that, I would never forget that first day when I received my first hug, and my first approval of being a beautiful person because, he indeed made me feel very special.

5

My First Crush

Our house was finally built. It took two years for the construction to be complete but, for us it had seemed like there was never an end. I guess we were just very anxious to be in something that was ours. The house was beautiful, and one of the best houses in the island. It was a one floor house with cathedral ceilings. Before moving in, we went to the house to see if everything was accessible. Our voices would echo as we talked to another. It felt kind of spooky. The house was well built, and the rooms were huge. The dining room along with the kitchen, and T.V. room were all out in the open.

I loved my bedroom. It was so big, and I was able to fit all my things and still have plenty of space. Sometimes after school, I would sit on my love seat and read a book, or dose off for a few minutes. I felt like some kind of millionaire who had the perfect house, and the perfect life.

This house was what my parents had dreamed of for such a long time. They were so excited, and thought they finally had the perfect life they've always been waiting for. Everything was running smooth like it always did, before another tragedy came into our lives.

While my father was outside mowing the larn, my mother decided to unpack the rest of the boxes that were still in the garage.

"Things are finally falling into place." She thought.

While my mother opened box after box and reached the last one, she noticed a package lying down right beside it. She picked it up, and suddenly remembered that it was something she received along time ago but, never had the chance to open it. When she had initially received it, she had put it aside and totally forgot about it. It didn't even phase her when she had packed for her departure to the Azores because, she was in such a hurry and had no time to double check things.

As my mother stared at the package, she noticed there was no return address. It was an anonymous package. As she brought it into the T.V. room, she opened it and to her surprise she pulled out a video tape with nothing written on it. My mother was curious to find out what it was, and decided to play it.

She was totally shocked in what she was viewing. It was a video based on that parish she attended before she had left her homeland.

"Oh, dear God." She cried.

"I just can't believe it! My husband was right all along!" My mother whispered.

She cried as she saw pastors from that parish in the sacristy kneeling down on the floor surrounding sacs filled with all of their parishioners money. They were all thrilled throwing money up in the air with such joyous faces.

"Well, I guess they paid no attention to the commandment of not stealing. They're going to rot in hell, that's for sure. I guess now I can say that I'm glad I moved here." My mother whispered.

My mother never told my father about the package because, she knew he would try ganging up on her. She knew exactly what he would say,

"See. I told you. They're all a bunch of phonies but, you didn't what to listen to me. You thought you were right and somebody else had to prove you wrong because you didn't believe me. I can't believe you can't even trust me after all these years of marriage."

My mother threw out the package, and put all of its content behind her. She was starting a new life now with her family, and didn't want to remember about those rotten times in the past that almost destroyed her marriage.

Another school year had begun for me, and I was so excited as usual. Not many of my friends from last year were in the same class as me but, I made new friends. Monica, Sonia, and Marisa were very nice girls, and very fun to be with. They'd make me laugh with their jokes, and their reactions when they would see a good-looking guy pass by.

"Oh, my God! Look at that hunk!" Marisa would stare.

"I'm in flames! I think I'm going to pass out." Sonia would get beat red.

"I'd love to throw myself in his arms, and melt like butter cause darn he's sizzling!" Monica's cravings for good-looking guys always exceeded her cravings of hunger.

"You girls are too much for me." I'd laugh.

I loved hanging out with them. They were a bunch of happy girls who just wanted to have fun. When my friends and I had a free class period, we would walk in the city. Our school was in the city, and there was a lot we could do and see in the city. There was a park. However, it wasn't just a park. It was more like a florist place than a park. There were different types of plants, trees and flowers. Also, several palm trees and a fountain as you walked in. For children, there were swings and an entertainment area. It was a nice place to relax after a long hard working day, or school day. My friends and I would go there several times to hang out, and talk about things other than school work.

Sometimes we'd walk in the city, and check out all of the little shops, and stores or sometimes we'd go pick up some food close by and sit on a porch from one of the little houses in front of our school. We were a good group of friends that cared a whole deal about each other. We were inseparable friends, and that's the way it should always be.

There was also a military camp located close by, and sometimes we'd take a bus there and would sneak in. We weren't supposed to be there but, we were crazy girls who just wanted to check out the good-looking Portuguese soldiers. Many times we'd see them jogging around the camp with their shirts off. They were hot! My friends and I once took one of the soldier's shirts, wet it, and placed a rose on top from a rosebush that was close by. When he came back for his shirt he started laughing and looking around to see if he found the person that had done that but, he had no luck because we hid behind a big tree close by.

Something bizarre must have happened in my first Portugese class. It felt like someone had done some kind witchcraft on my teacher to curse me. Now why in the world, did she put me in a group of all boys when there were so many girls? Was there a reason?

My group was a group of four. I worked with Pedro, George, Tiago, and Bruno. Unfortunately, they picked me as the writer despite my difficulties in writing. Bruno out of the bunch, was very sweet. He would come up to me once in a while, and check if I was writing the assignment correctly. If he noticed there was a mistake, he'd explain to me what was wrong, and would correct it for me. I liked the way he would approach me, and see how I was doing with the writing. I liked his sweet smile, and his blue eyes. I'd also like when he'd get closer to me, and read my paper. For some reason, he seemed to interest me. He seemed to interest me a whole lot.

He was a scrawny looking thing, short, with black hair and blue eyes. His glasses made him look like a short professor, and his big lips sort of looked like fish lips. However, his looks didn't target me as much as his personality. As days and weeks passed by, I became more and more attracted to him. He was my first crush.

The funniest part of it all was that Bruno hung out with these two guys that my friends Sonia, and Monica had crushes on. Sonia had a crush on Tiago. Monica had a crush on Paul, and I had a crush on Bruno. We liked a group of guys that also hung out together.

Many times when we had free class periods, we would watch them play basketball on the school courtyard. After a while, I think they came to suspicions about us. Whenever the ball bounced toward us, we would sometimes tease them in not wanting to give them the basketball until one of them would come up to us, and beg for the basketball.

When they were in the library studying, we would be there too. We'd pick a table right in front of them to study, and to take a few glances here and there. When they were in the library we could never concentrate on our studies.

We would get so distracted looking at our sweethearts, laughing and giggling about things we would say back and forth. Several times the librarian would kick us out because, we would make too much noise. Although they were studying, they knew we were talking about them and would give us a little smile here and there.

My friend Anna from my 8th grade class knew where Bruno lived. On a Friday I had a short school schedule, and so I asked Anna to show me his residence. He lived in the city projects, and on his clothes line his mother had hung up his washed underwear. Anna and I started laughing.

"Jenny, look at your sweetheart's underwear! Now you know what underwear to buy him if you marry him. Red polka-dotted undies!" Anna laughed so hard.

I could barely hold my laughter and on top of it all, I was getting feverish hot flashes. You might think I was undergoing an early menopause. From that day on, we started calling Bruno "UNDER-PANTS" when we talked about him among the four of us including Anna.

I was so glad when Friday's came around because, school wasn't all that easy. It was basically college level material, and some of the days were so long. Some days I would start at eight in the morning, and come home at six in the evening. It was tough for all us students.

The good part was that there were no substitute teachers. When a teacher was absent, we would have that whole hour to ourselves. Sometimes I'd get lucky because, it would so happen to be my last class and I'd go home earlier.

In the summer, there was always a lot going on in this island. There were street bullfights, and feasts all season long. Each town had their own street bullfight and feast. I liked to go to both. I'd go to the bullfights most of the time with my cousin Monica, and her friend Carla. We would always have plenty of fun together. Fun checking out all of the good-looking men.

Many single girls would go to the bullfights to encounter the man of their dreams. Male attraction. In other words, they went to find themselves a boyfriend, and not because they were interested in the bullfight. Bullfights were a good way to meet many guys. Single and married men would be on the street teasing the bull while single and married women would be watching from their or their neighbor's porch.

On a Saturday while I was still lying in bed and thinking of Bruno as I laughed by my lonesome, the phone rang.

"Jennifer. It's for you." My mother shouted.

"Hello?" I asked.

"Hey, Jenny. It's your cousin Monica. How are you?" Monica asked.

"I'm fine. What about you?"

"Ok. I guess. Hey, I was wondering if you'd like to go to the bullfight at Porto Judeu with Carla and I."

"Yeah. Why not? What time?" I asked.

"I'll pick you up at eleven o'clock because, it starts at twelve." Monica replied.

"Sounds good! I'll be ready." I replied.

Sure enough. Monica was at my house at eleven o'clock. When we arrived at Porto Judeu, there were lots of people waiting for the bullfight to begin. Everyone's porches were swamped with people. Many neighbors would have a table set up with appetizers, and drinks for company. There would also be men outside selling ice cream, pistachios, and chips.

My cousin, her friend, and I bought pistachios, and were eating them as they waited for the entertainment to begin. While we were waiting and looking around, we noticed a group of good-looking guys standing below the porch we were on. What do you think we did? Monica, Carla, and I started throwing pistachio shells at their heads to get their attention.

We'd throw them harder, and harder until they finally looked up. For some reason I duck down. I didn't want them to see me. I always felt insecure about meeting new people, especially guys because I was afraid of what they'd think of me. I had known that for Mario it didn't matter that I had a defect but, what were my chances of finding someone like him again. I hid myself behind the little brick fence around the porch as I saw my cousin, and Carla waving and smiling at them.

"Why can't I find the courage to do the same? Why do I let myself image bother me so much?" I'd told myself.

I guess, I belittled myself too much. It wasn't my fault that I was born with this defect. However, I had a really hard time accepting that especially when I was around guys.

"What happened to you, girl? I thought you were never going to get up from that corner." Monica questioned me as I came up.

"Why didn't you stay up here with us, and meet the nice looking guys?" Monica questioned me again.

"I'm not pretty enough to impress them. They'd probably laugh at me." I bowed my head.

"No. They wouldn't, Jenny! Just because you have that defect doesn't mean you're not a pretty girl." Monica replied.

"Yeah. Well I don't feel that way about myself. Tell me. What's the first thing that attracts men? Isn't it the looks? It's all about the looks!" I replied.

"Jenny. Don't say that. Mario was very interested in you, so it seemed." Monica tried to cheer me up.

"Yeah! One in a million! What are my chances of finding someone like him who had looked at my insides before looking at my self image?" I abruptly wiped my tears.

The owner of the house saw me in tears, and approached me.

"My! My! My! No one cries in my house!" She told me.

"Oh, it's nothing really. She just had a nervous breakdown when she saw her boyfriend hug another girl." Monica lied.

"There's no reason to cry, my dear. If I were you, I'd slap him silly." Mrs. Santos replied.

After the bull fight was over, I thanked Monica for lying as we walked to the car.

"Gee. You're a good liar! Thanks for keeping my personal issues between us."

"Anytime. Jenny. Anytime." Monica gave me a hug.

Every town also had there own feast for a week, and their own street bullfight. Some towns would contact a DJ, and every night there would be entertainment. Many people would dance on the street, and there were several people with carts selling drinks, ice creams, and any kind of snack you could possibly think of.

The city had a much bigger feast. They called it the "Sanjoaninhas." For a whole week they'd have so much entertainment. They would have all different kinds of rides, a Ferris wheel, and a carousel. Every night there were concerts from famous Portugese singers, and bands. The first day, they would have a parade to introduce the queen of the city that year. The parade consisted of many groups of people with very colorful garments. They also had floats dressed up in satin that were so nicely decorated. The following day consisted groups of people from all the towns in Terceira. Each town had their own special, and colorful garments. They also had their own dance. As they would walk down the main street of the city called "Rua Da Se," ladies and their partners would sing and dance. The following day they would have children from each town dance and sing dressed in their colorful garments.

Many tourists from around the world would come to see this feast. If one wanted a good seat, he or she would have to go there about two hours earlier because thousands of people went and see this feast. Many cafe's, and restaurants in the city would make a lot of business during this week. My parents and I loved going to this feast. Sometimes some of my friends would be in a dance, and I'd talk to them as they passed by. Sometimes my parents stood for the fire works by the ocean. Everyone had such a good time in this feast because, there was always so much to do and see.

Winters were much more quiet. My mother was home most of the time bored out of her mind but, she always managed to find things to keep her busy. Nobody wanted to offer her a job because, she couldn't read or write. Most of the time she watched Spanish soap operas. She was addicted to them, and couldn't miss one episode or else she'd be devastated. She also occupied herself with house work. This house of ours was no small house. It took her two days to clean the entire house.

On the other hand, my father loved his job as a security guard. He would guard a milk factory at night, and while he worked he listened to the radio. My mother would sometimes dedicate songs for him, and he'd start smiling as he listened to her voice on the radio.

"She's always with me." My father would laugh.

One early morning before my father's shift was over, he noticed an employee carrying out two jugs of wine. My father approached the man, and questioned him.

"What's in those jugs, sir?" He asked.

"Wine." The employee replied.

"How could you have gotten wine from a milk factory?" My father questioned him again.

The man knew he was discovered, and got so mad. He ended up opening the jugs, and pouring all of the milk on the grass. My father felt so proud, and told his supervisor about his discovery.

When I started 10th grade, I was finally being assigned to a Portugese tutor but, it didn't help me much. I was just learning things that were of least importance.

I had the same Portuguese teacher that I had in 8th grade, and when she passed out the corrected tests she called me up to her desk.

"Jennifer, your writing has improved incredibly! I'm very proud of you. All you need to focus on now is the material." My teacher smiled.

Although I had failed the test, I was happy to know that I had made a great achievement. I was determined to take that next step. I wanted to pass the year to be with all of my friends, especially Bruno.

Many times Bruno would come up to me, and talk with me or joke around with me. He made me laugh and smile, and helped me with school work when difficulty arose. He meant a lot to me and besides, I liked all his attention. I loved when he'd look at me all seriously. I loved his walk and his talk. And most of all, I'd love when he'd come up to me and start a conversation with me. When he'd come up to me, my heart would beat ten times faster, and I'd get all flush with fever. I had never felt this way for anyone. I liked Mario a whole lot. Don't get me wrong! However, what I felt for Bruno seemed much stronger, and much more alive within my heart. When he'd smile at me, my insides would melt. Despite how I felt, I doubted Bruno would ever feel the same way for me. I was probably not his type of girl.

My friends loved to play around with me, and make me laugh. They knew what would trigger my laughter.

"We know why you like Bruno so much. It's because you saw his underwear!" They would say.

"What color were they?" They questioned me.

I'd get beat red, and couldn't respond because if I did, I knew I'd burst out laughing. After a moment or two I replied,

"They were red polka-dotted ones." I laughed so hard that I almost ended up wetting my pants. My friends laughed too. We were a bunch of crazy girls.

The guys in our class loved to tease us, girls especially me because, I was short and petite. They'd love pulling our bras. That was their pet peeve. George would freak me out when he'd pick me up, and hold me above the railing to the staircase. It was a three-floor building, and if I so happened to fall, I wouldn't have been alive. I knew he was only playing around, but I still fought with him several times about it until he finally realized I was right. I knew he would have been devastated if he so happened to lose his grip, and I ended up falling.

Instead, he would pick me up, and would run around the corridor carrying me in his arms. I'd get aggravated sometimes but, I have to admit that I actually liked all of this attention. Sometimes I'd be talking to a friend, and then all of a sudden I would be lifted. My friends would start laughing as George took me for a ride. School was so much fun out here. We were all friends, and we were like family.

My paternal grandfather had a very severe case of asthma, and the humid air here didn't help him much either. Many times he'd end up going to the emergency room, and would get admitted. My cousin Monica and I would take turns sleeping over our grand-mother's house because, she was afraid of being by herself in such a big house.

Every time I'd sleep over, she'd drive me crazy! She'd feed me to death and if I refused to eat all that was on my plate, she'd throw a fit. When it was sleep time, I'd try to adjust to her brick mattress. She'd tell me the harder the mattress was, the better it was for the back. Just when I'd finally get comfortable, she'd start snoring. She'd snore so loud that I'd have to put my pillow over my head. Then after a while she'd wake up, and tell me that I was making too much noise, and that she couldn't sleep. She'd blame me, when it was her all along.

On a Sunday morning while I was at my grandmother's house, I experienced an earthquake. I was lying on my cousin Liz's bed read-ing a magazine when all of a sudden, I felt the bed rocking back and forth. A few seconds later, I hear my grandmother yell out my name. I rushed down the stairs in panic as I saw everything moving back and forth. We both evacuated the house immediately. While I was outside, I saw my aunt's house, and many other houses on that street rock back and forth. However, my aunt's house didn't rock as much as most of those houses on that street. Most of those houses were very old, and made of rock and sand. Luckily, the earthquake only lasted for about two minutes, and there was no damage. In those moments, I just wanted to hug my grandmother. Although she'd drive me nuts sometimes, I still loved her.

After a while my parents knew something was going on. I was constantly laughing in my bedroom by myself, and was always so happy. Happy in a way they've never seen.

"What's up with you, Jennifer? Lately you've been laughing by yourself in your bedroom, and singing in the shower." My mother asked.

My father turned around and said,

"Oh, it must be because of her boyfriend."

"Is that true?" My mother asked me.

"No. I do like this guy in my class but, we're not boyfriend and girlfriend." I responded.

"Forget about boys, and think about your studies. Men are nothing but trouble." My mother told me.

"What?" My father was upset.

"Not you, honey. Sorry. I meant most men, and not all." My mother corrected herself as she smiled and gave my father a luscious kiss.

This Tuesday Bruno sat right beside me. I loved every second. He put his arm around me, and started talking to me. I was nervous, and unstable but beneath all of that nervousness I was able to keep my jungle of love under control. As he got closer, my urge to kiss him grew stronger, and stronger. However, I was able to keep my cool.

I started wearing skirts to grab his attention. Most of the time I'd catch him sitting on the floor melting to the core as he checked me out. Sometimes I'd look him straight in the eye and smile. Other times I'd just get shy, and would blush.

After a while when I noticed that I had his attention, I started lifting my skirts a bit higher every time I wore a skirt until it became a mini skirt. I thought he wouldn't notice, or any of the other guys in my class but, I was wrong. It's funny how men notice such things in women. It wasn't a drastic change. I didn't go from long right to mini. I did it gradually.

On a Friday, our history teacher was lecturing about women's rights, and how women started lifting the hems of their skirts higher and higher. Bruno started laughing and said,

"Like Jenny!"

All of the guys in my class started laughing because, they knew it was true. I was so embarrassed, and couldn't even look at my teacher but, that didn't stop me from wearing skirts. Yet, I wonder if Bruno was suspicious of me liking him more than just a friend. He'd get me confused. Sometimes I felt like he knew, and sometimes I felt like he didn't.

One day in gym class, he lifted his shirt and rubbed his scrawny white belly as he looked directly at me with a smile on his face. My friends were talking to me and I didn't have the slightest idea what they were talking about because, I was just focused on him.

When the first semester was over, my mother and I went to a parent teacher conference to pick up my grades. My friends were there, and I introduced them to my mother. As I was standing in line talking to my friends, I mentioned Bruno.

"Did you girls see what he did in gym class? He's so sweet." I told my friends. "Please! Girl! That scrawny looking thing!" Marisa was joking.

A minute later, the woman in front of us turned around.

"Hi, I'm Bruno's mother." The lady introduced herself.

I just couldn't believe it. I was standing in front of Bruno's mother. Marisa was so embarrassed because, of what she had said but, there was no need for her to be upset because Bruno's mother was a very nice lady.

"Hi. My name is Jennifer, these are my friends, and this is my mother." I introduced everyone.

"Oh, so you must be the famous Jennifer my son keeps talking about." The lady smiled.

Gee, I never thought Bruno ever thought of me or mentioned me to anyone. This meant a lot to me, and made me feel happy to know that I was special to him. Bruno's mother seemed to like my mother. They both chit chatted back and forth while we waited for our turn with the teacher. It was such a coincidence that my mother met the mother of the guy I liked, when there were so many mothers there that night.

There was this girl in my class named Tanya who thought she was all it, and it seemed to me that she had great interest in Bruno. Besides her interest in Bruno, he wasn't the only one in her bunch. She was a type of Barbie doll who thought she could have any man she wanted, and darn that killed me when she would be around Bruno. When I'd see her sitting on the edge of his desk flirting with him, I'd get jealous. However, I could tell that he didn't care for her any way because, he'd brush her off all the time. I still hated it though because, I wanted him to be mine.

When Valentine's day came around, my friend Anna did something I just couldn't believe. She sent Bruno a love letter pretending to be me. It was an anonymous letter, thanks to God. In the letter she wrote that I loved him, and if he didn't like me that way it was because he was nothing but a fool. I couldn't believe she did that! I was so mad. I'd never call anyone a fool for not loving me.

Anna told me about the letter while we were playing basketball on the school courtyard and boy, I started playing really well when she was telling me everything. I played so well that my friends couldn't even believe it. I was never good at any sports but, today my madness motivated me into playing like an athlete.

"Jenny!" Anna would say in surprise as I took the ball off her hands.

"Why did you do that?" I argued.

"He had to know, Jenny." Anna responded.

"I knew he had to know but, I was the one who wanted to tell him." I replied.

"Sorry, Jenny." Anna replied.

"Sorry for nothing." I pretended to be furious.

I wasn't about to break our friendship over some stupid letter. Although, I liked to see her reaction when I pretended to look mad.

The next day when we were playing basketball, I saw Bruno lying down with his head against a pole constantly staring at me.

"He thinks it's I described in that letter, most definitely." I thought.

I just had to straighten this out. I wasn't going to let this stay like this.

The next day I dragged my friend Anna where they were playing, and started fighting with her out loud so they could hear.

"Why did you write him that letter?" I shouted.

"Jenny, because you like him." Anna was surprised.

"There was no need for you to put your nose where it doesn't belong." I replied.

After a while, Anna caught on. She knew that I wasn't seriously mad at her but just wanted to make the scene because, I wanted Bruno to know that I wasn't the one who wrote him that letter.

"How could I trust you now? You revealed my precious secret, and now everyone probably knows. Thanks to you!" I said as I was just about to laugh. Bruno and his friends started laughing. However, that letter didn't cause no harm to our friendship. He never mentioned anything about me liking him and neither did I.

I loved every bit of my life, and had every thing I needed. I seemed to have the perfect life, and thought I had it all. I thought that things would always be easier and pain free for me from now on, and thought my suffering days would be over but, little did I know what was in store for me down the road.

6

Darkness

As winter approached of the year 1998, I came down with a severe cold and cough. Usually after a week or two weeks, any healthy person gets better due to a good immune system but for me it took much longer than that. Only after about a month my cold started getting better. However, being ill wasn't over for me.

Once my cold and cough were gone, I thought I was back to normal like any other healthy person but, I was totally mistaken. My energy level decreased to almost nothing. My friends would want to go walk in the city but, I would be too tired to go. I'd tell them to go have fun, and that maybe tomorrow I'd feel more energetic but, there was never a tomorrow when I had felt better.

In gym class I couldn't run much because, I'd start grasping for air as if I had an asthma problem. One day my gym teacher pulled me out of the jogging bunch, and asked me if I had asthma problems. I told him,

"Not that I know of, Mr. Santos."

"Well, I seriously think you should get that checked." My gym teacher replied.

When I got home that day, I told my mother what my teacher had told me. "Jennifer. You don't have asthma. Your teacher doesn't know what he's talking about. Just because he pushes you kids too much, doesn't mean that everyone can do it." My mother replied.

I didn't say anything, and just went to my room to get some rest. Lately, I was needing lots of rest. I knew things weren't right. I knew I wasn't myself lately, and knew that something was coming on. I wasn't that energetic happy person anymore. I was always tired and weak.

At first I thought that maybe I had been so tired because of school, and studying. I told my mother about me feeling tired and weak all the time, and she told me that it was probably because I studied too much, and wasn't getting enough vitamins to keep me going. She bought me multivitamins and I took them but, everything seemed the same and actually grew worse. I then started getting constant migraines. I'd take acetaminophen every single day to relieve me from the headaches but, they would consistently come back. A couple of days later, I started getting sores on the roof of my mouth. It hurt so much especially when I would eat and because of this, I hardly ate.

On the week of finals, I woke up and prompted myself. As I walked to the bus stop, I kept grasping for air. One step for me was as if I jogged a mile. As I was half way there, I felt like I was going to pass out and leaned against a neighbor's fence. As I walked again, a neighbor stopped me.

"Where do you think you're going in this condition?" Alex asked me.

"I have to catch the bus because, I have a final today." I told him as I leaned against the fence and grasped for air.

"Oh, no. You're not going to school in this condition. I'm walking you home this instant. You need to rest." Alex was concerned.

Rest. Rest. Rest. That's all I did, and I still wasn't getting any better. In school at lunch time, I'd barely eat anything, and my friends started worrying about me.

"Jenny, girl! You have to eat! You're letting yourself down." Sonia would tell me.

"I can't eat, Sonia. I have sores in my mouth that hurt so much when I eat." I told her.

"I know Jenny but, you need to force yourself and you need to get checked. Look at you! You're becoming anorexic! For Christ's sake! I'm worried about you girl, and I'm not prepared to lose my best friend." Sonia was worried about me.

I gave her a hug and wept.

"I don't know what's happening to me! I was fine last year, and now this year has brought me hell." I cried.

My friend was right. I was letting myself down by not resting as much as I should have. I was a study freak that wanted to get good grades, and would force myself to study even when I wasn't feeling good. I should have been forcing myself to eat, and not forcing myself to study. I would always take school and studying seriously, and because of my stress of being responsible for getting good grades, I was letting my health slip away.

I got to the point where I couldn't even concentrate any more as I studied. I'd get so nervous and uptight about everything that was happening to me, especially because I was unable to study as much due to the fact that I needed more rest. I was so sick of being sick. This seemed to be a constant thing in my life now.

My father's cousin Maria had the Holy Ghost in her house, and she invited us to pray and be in her procession. The Holy Ghost was a Portuguese tradition. For seven weeks a crown that represented a crown blessed by the Holy Spirit was sent to a person's house for a week. Maria's name was picked out of the basket, and she was able to bring the crown home for a week followed by her procession on the last day.

Usually the person, who brought the crown home, would make an altar decorated with lots of flowers, and would put the crown in the middle of the altar. Neighbors and family would sing and pray the rosary in front of the altar, and then after there were beverages and appetizers.

Sunday was the big procession. I was entitled to carry the big red flag with the dove on it. It was a heavy flag and because I was so weak, I had no clue how I was going to carry that flag for about a mile. In addition, I had high heels on. Before we started walking, I asked the Lord to help me.

After we finished the walk, I was stunned. I couldn't believe that I was able to walk that mile carrying that heavy flag in the condition I was in. It was as if God carried the flag for me. At that moment, I knew God was with me and had always been by my side helping get through the days. My sister Monique was one of the little girls getting crowned. During the mass the priest placed the crown on top of her head, and blessed her with Holy water. She wore a white cute little dress with her hair up and her curls draping down. She looked so pretty.

After the procession, I just wanted to go home because, I was so tired. However, Maria had made food for us to eat, and so we had lunch there. I didn't eat much because, everything I ate would hurt my sores.

While my father drove us home, he flipped out on me.

"Why didn't you eat anything, and why did you act so stupid in front of everyone?" My father argued.

"I wasn't acting. I'm sick!" I replied.

"You're not sick. You just want attention. That's what you want!" My father replied.

After that I made no further remark because, I knew he was mad. My father was a very unrealistic man. Things had to hit him in the face for him to believe it. My mother on the other end, never said a word. She knew I was right. She knew from the start that I was getting sick. The reason she never said anything was because, she wanted to keep peace in the family.

I was hurt because I knew how I was feeling inside, and my father just couldn't reason that I was seriously sick. It got to the point when I couldn't sleep at night anymore. I'd have hallucinations of a man raising an ax against me to kill me. I felt as if someone had put a curse on me, but who? Everyone liked me. I don't know! All I know is that I'd see this man with an ax over my bed, and I'd start crying. I was also having trouble breathing at night, and had to use three pillows while I slept so I could breathe.

The only concrete answer to these hallucinations I was experiencing was because of a murder that occurred to the next door neighbor's daughter a few weeks ago. Her husband had crushed some sleeping pills, and had put it in her drink. Then after she was asleep, he took her body to the woods and killed her with an ax. I guess because of all the problems I was facing, and because I felt lifeless and as if death was calling me, this came to my mind. I'd cover myself with my blankets and would cry and scream with so much fright because of this man I kept seeing over my bed with an ax.

My mother started getting very worried as she saw me getting weaker and weaker, and seeing my weight drop drastically. Sometimes she'd take a wooden spoon, and force me to eat by threatening me that she'd hit me if I didn't.

"I can't eat because my sores hurt so much!" I cried.

"I know honey, but you need to eat! Your letting yourself get worse." My mother replied.

"I can't, mom! I just can't!" I wept.

My mother was so nervous. I could tell. She knew something was wrong. After a while, she would end up making me some creamy oatmeal so I could eat. At least this was something I could swallow.

"I'm taking you to the doctor's office tomorrow." My mother cried as she looked at me.

The following day I went and see my primary care physician, and explained to him what was going on.

"I've been having shortness of breath, constant headaches, sours in my mouth, fatigue, weakness, and mild fevers." I told him.

He then told me that I could only get x-rays done in about a week.

"This is ridiculous! She could be dying, and the closest appointment is within a week!" My mother was furious.

"Sorry, madam. I can't do anything about it!" The doctor replied.

As we walked to the car, I grasped for air. My mother then turned around and said,

"You know what, Andrew? I'm going to take our daughter to the emergency room right now! I'm not going to wait any longer because, the longer we wait the worse she gets."

My parents took me to the emergency room and promised me that they would find out what was wrong, and that I would soon be back to normal. Well, it didn't turn out as peachy as they expected. It all boiled down to some serious, and severe stuff.

We waited so long for me to get checked out but, in the long run it was so worth it because I was seriously ill. They first performed an EKG, and then an ultrasound on my heart. As they performed the ultrasound, they noticed that the sac around my heart was enlarged. They then called a cardiologist immediately to verify their finding. The cardiologist then made a final diagnosis based on my heart condition, and told my parents that I would need to stay at the hospital for further observation and investigation because, the fluids that were accumulating in the sac of my heart had to be brought on because of a disease. In order to find that disease, I'd need to stay in the hospital for further analysis.

"I'd like to tell both of you that you are very lucky your daughter is still alive. Her heart has been suffocated due to these fluids compressing against it, and would eventually stop beating at any time in this stage. I'm so glad she came in today, and I promise we'll make every effort to find the leading cause of this abnormality." The cardiologist gave his sympathy.

"Please, I beg you! Help my daughter!" My mother cried.

My father was speechless as I lie helplessly on the hospital bed. His head was down, and tears rolled down as he wept silently. As they took me to my room, I waved to my parents and cried because I was so scared. What if I wouldn't make it tomorrow? If I didn't, I'd never see them again.

In the morning I woke up, and thanked God for still being alive. They drew my blood, and realized I had severe anemia, which in my case was the lack of red blood cells. When my parents came and visit me, my mother noticed that a pint of blood was connected to me. She called the nurse.

"Call my daughter's doctor this instant! I'd like to speak with him!" My mother was ticked off.

"Yes. Mrs. Wright. How can I help you?" The doctor asked.

"Don't I have to sign an informed consent before you administer blood to my daughter?" My mother was angry.

"We don't do that here." The doctor replied.

"What do you mean, you don't do that here?! What kind of hospital is this? In the United States we always sign a consent for any medical procedure." My mother told him.

"If you want, I can discontinue the transfusion right now and let your daughter die!" My doctor was furious.

"No!" My mother screamed.

"She's not going to die!" My mother shouted.

"I can assure you that all of our pints of blood have been tested for AIDS and other blood transmitted diseases. Does that make you more comfortable?" The doctor asked.

"Yes. I'm sorry. It's just that I have so much on my plate right now." My mother cried.

"I understand, Mrs. Wright. I have a daughter too and if something happened like this to her, I don't know how I would react." The doctor was compassionate.

As the days passed by, I just grew worse. Transfusions weren't helping because after my blood count boosted up, it would then go back down to where it was. No matter how many efforts they made to get rid of the fluids around my heart, they kept on accumulating. I still wasn't eating much because the sores in my mouth were getting worse, and worse. My feet and hands started swelling up with fluids due to kidney dysfunction. I had gotten to the point that I couldn't even sleep in bed because, I was so uncomfortable. My feet looked like big Portuguese rolls, and my hands looked like I had severe mumps. I couldn't put socks or slippers on because, it would stay tight and hurt due to the swelling. My feet and hands would hurt so much, and I would end up sleeping on the recliner that was in my room.

I was getting weaker by the minute and got to the point that I couldn't get up on top of my bed. I couldn't get in the shower, and needed someone to help me wash myself. It seemed to me like these doctors weren't doing anything for me. They tried everything according to their knowledge but nothing seemed to work mainly because, they couldn't figure out what was causing all of this.

A few days later, a specialist from Lisbon, Portugal came to my room and examined me. He was a young doctor but, he knew his stuff. He was a very friendly, and compassionate doctor. He would spend sometime with me while I told him how I felt, and how I was scared about dying. While I was in the hospital, I drew a picture of a house with many flowers and palm trees. It was a drawing expressing my wanting of a normal and natural life. When I completed the drawing, I gave it to him and he smiled.

"Thank you, Jennifer. I will always keep this because, it will always remind me of you. I'm going to have a little talk with your parents now. Then I'll come back to talk with you about what needs to be done for you to get better." The doctor told me.

"Okay, I'll be waiting." I smiled.

Dr. Mendes the specialist, approached my parents.

"Hello. I'm Dr. Mendes. You must be Jennifer's parents. Right?" The doctor asked.

"Yes." My mother replied.

"Your daughter is a very fascinating young lady but, I'm afraid she is probably not going to make it. I want to transfer her to Lisbon Hospital immediately for the sake of her life. She needs dialysis immediately because, she is drowning herself due kidney failure, and at any point in time she may undergo congestive heart failure as well." The doctor was worried.

"Can't I just take her to Boston, Massachusetts?" My mother questioned the doctor.

"I'm afraid she won't make it. Her case is urgent, and she needs to be treated as soon as possible." The doctor insisted.

Dr. Mendes came back and told me that I was going to Lisbon Hospital so I could get better, and also told me that my mother was coming with me which made me feel more comfortable. Although my father wanted to accompany us, he stood in Terceira because of his job. As the ambulance took me and my mother along with my doctor to the airport, I could see my father and sister outside crying so much. It was a very emotional and hurtful moment for both me and my mother but, it was for my sake and for my survival.

When the ambulance arrived at the airport, they put me on a wheelchair and ramped me up to the airplane. As soon as we arrived, I was brought by ambulance to the hospital and as soon as I entered the hospital, I was immediately sent to the operating room.

There they gave me some novocaine to numb my chest. I screamed so loud with so much pain as they injected the numbing medication on my chest. Then they made a pericardial window, which is a tiny hole in the sac of my heart to drain out the fluids. There they stuck a fine tube, and I could see the liquid draining into a silver bowl. After that procedure, they brought me to the intensive care unit where I was put on continuous hemodialysis for a week to get rid of the excess fluid I had on me, and toxins my kidneys weren't filtering out.

They had to place a feeding tube down my throat, and all I ingested were liquids. They basically gave me Ensure shakes in order for me to get all the vitamins my body needed. Doctors worked feverishly on me to find out my diagnosis but, they were unsuccessful. After doing everything they could do on me, they lost hope and called my mother in the doctor's conference room.

"Miranda." The doctor paused.

"I strongly advise you to bring your husband here because, there are very minimal expectancies of your daughter surviving." The doctor commented.

My mother cried so hard. She felt as if her heart was getting ripped out of her chest. After she stopped crying, she came and see me. Before she went in, she looked at me through the window of the unit's door, and cried as she saw my helpless body all hooked up to various medical equipment. It was as if I were in a coma. I was hooked up to oxygen, a heart monitor, dialysis tubing where my blood was being filtered continuously, a urinary catheter, and a feeding tube because I couldn't eat on my own.

"Mom! What took you so long?" I could barely speak.

"I was just talking to your doctor." My mother replied as she forced herself to hold her tears back.

"Oh." I smiled.

"Jennifer. Tomorrow I won't be able to come because, I have to go get your father and sister." My mother told me.

"But tomorrow is my birthday. I don't want to have a birthday alone." I was worried and sad.

"I know, sweety. I know but, I have to go get your father. I promise you that the next day I'll be here bright and early. I promise." My mother smiled as she tried covering her urge to cry, and ran her fingers through my hair.

That night I prayed. I prayed for God to have mercy on my soul, and save me from death. I guess I was a bit loud because, one of the nurses came in to check on me. I told her I was okay, and that I was just praying. She smiled at me before returning to the nurse's station.

The next day June 10 of 1999, I woke up with a surprise. The nurses of the unit came in my room and sang Happy Birthday. One of the nurses was holding a plate with a big cupcake that had a candle. After they finished singing, I blew the candle and made a wish. I made a wish for life. Then I smiled, and thanked them. That was very thoughtful of them. They made me feel special.

The following day my parents went to see me. They were both crying in separate corners because, the doctor had told them to expect the worse.

I knew why they were crying because, I could sense it.

"What? Is this my funeral?" I asked as tears came down my face.

My parents couldn't speak. They were just too hurt to respond to my question.

When my father had seen me at first, he was in total shock when he saw how bad I was. As he gave me a kiss, he cried. I could feel his tears coming down my cheek. They both told me how much they loved me, and I told them how much I loved them too, and that I was sorry if I ever hurt them or made them angry. I asked for forgiveness even though they told me that I never did anything wrong. It hurt me so much to see them suffer over me. Sometimes I felt as if I were a burden to them.

Everyone thought there was no hope in me living. Doctors lost hope, and my parents had no where else to turn except facing reality. I at this point wasn't worried at all. I left everything in God's hands. If it was my time to go, he'd take me but if not, he would miraculously save me.

What would be my destination? Death or survival? As my mother cried, she suddenly remembered about this lady she had meant a while ago who was selling crochet butterfly magnets. This lady was the sister of the construction owner that had built our house. She was recently diagnosed with Lupus, and was selling these butterflies for donations to the Lupus Foundation. After this thought, my mother approached my doctor and asked if I had been tested for Tuberculous or Lupus? My doctor then tested me for Tuberculous and Systemic Lupus and after a second try, I came up positive for Systemic Lupus. Once they received the results, they started treating me right away. They started me on Prednisone, and Cytoxan. The doctor told my parents that Cytoxan was a form of chemotherapy that would help bring the sickness into remission, and also help heal my kidneys. If it wasn't for that person my mother had meant, and if it wasn't for my mother, I would've died. It seemed like God had it all planned. He had planned the encounter of this lady, and had reminded my mother of the purpose of that encounter in order to save my life.

After a couple of weeks, I started getting better and my kidneys started functioning again. Although my arms were all black and blue, what mattered to me was that I was still alive. My moderately dysfunctional mitral heart valve caused by the compression of fluids towards my heart was also healing, and in a few weeks I was ready to transfer back to the hospital in Terceira in order for me to finish recuperating.

I had been in the hospital for three months. Three scary months between life and death. There were times when I was very ill, and unconscious that I didn't even know where I was. Because I had been bedridden for three months, I needed to learn how to walk again and strengthen my muscles on my legs. After I was out of danger and finally home, my primary care doctor referred me to a Nephrologist, which is a doctor that specializes in kidney disease. There were no Lupus specialists in Terceira, and so my doctor had advised my parents about moving back to America where medical technology was more advanced.

7

Coping

My first appointment with my Nephrologist was scheduled, and there many questions my parents and I had. What was this disease? How could I have caught it? Is it a disease that I can control and live with? I hoped within time I could adjust to this disease. I knew there are going to be changes, that's for sure

Although my parents were with me, I was nervous as I walked into the doctor's office. Pattie, one of the medical assistants greeted me and had me take a seat while she took my vital signs. She was a short butterball, with long brown hair that was nicely wrapped into a bun. Besides her peachy appearance, she was a very sweet person. Pat made every attempt for my parents and I to feel comfortable. She was a doll. I guess the saying, "Good things come in small packages" is true.

After vital signs were taken, I was moved to another seat. Sandy, their phlebotomist drew my blood. She seemed to be very sweet too. After my blood was drawn, my parents and I were brought into the doctor's office.

"So, this must be courageous Jennifer and her parents." Dr. Teresa proudly commented.

I smiled at her as she smiled back. I didn't know where to begin my questioning. I had so many questions, and hoped I'd remember them all. My parents had questions too. They didn't know where to begin either but, there was no need to get frustrated because Dr. Teresa started the conversation.

"I know you, and your parents must have tons of questions for me. I will try my very best to answer them but, I'd like to assure you that this disease is not my speciality and think it would be best if your parents move back to your homeland for you to get treated by someone who does specialize in your disease. Right now you are stable but, there are many things that can flare it up again, and sometimes it can flare up on it's own. It's a disease that has a mind of it's own." Dr. Teresa explained.

"What is Systemic Lupus?" My mother asked.

"It's an autoimmune disease. We all have antibodies that help us fight colds or whatever foreign bodies inside us that cause illness. However, in a person with Systemic Lupus these antibodies think that the body's own flesh and organs are the foreign bodies, and these antibodies attack one's own organs. Systemic Lupus is the worse form of Lupus. There is another type of Lupus that's also very common which occurs on the skin. People with this Lupus tend to have flares on their skin such as rashes rather than their organs like in Systemic Lupus. In Jennifer's case, it attacked her heart, kidneys, and lungs. Luckily her kidney function is back to normal, and her heart and lungs are okay. She does however still have a leaky mitral valve due to the flare."

"Are there any precautions she must take?" My mother asked.

"Yes. Most definitely stay away from the sun. This is one main cause of flares. Limit stress loads. Exhaustion can also cause a flare. Be persistent with medications. If you slack on taking your medications, this can also cause a flare. One major sign that a Lupus flare is initiating is a Butterfly Rash on a person's face."

"A butterfly rash?" I asked.

"It looks like butterfly." The doctor replied.

"That's strange." I winked my eyes.

"You my dear, are a strong beautiful butterfly. God gave you wings to fly beyond your problems and live again because I have to tell you, very few survive what you survived. You are a designed **Metal Butterfly**. You're **strong as Metal**, and **beautiful as a Butterfly**." Dr. Teresa proudly replied.

I smiled. I understood what she was saying, and could picture it in my mind. I with such beautiful wings soaring away from tragedy, and trying to find happiness and salvation. Those words, God gave you wings to fly, made me realize how lucky I was to still be alive. It made me realize how much God loves me, and also made me feel special.

"Here is a list of all your medications you were taking in the hospital, and that you must take every day. You're also going to need a six-month trial of Cytoxan treatments, which is a type of chemotherapy. It's a one hour treatment done intravenously once a month. The purpose of this treatment is to put your sickness in remission, and to help heal your kidneys of any inflammation." Dr. Teresa explained.

After we left the doctor's office, my parents and I still had no idea of what this disease was, and still had many questions. A few days later my mother called her friend Sharon in America, and asked her if she could find a book with information on Lupus. After about a month, we received a package from her that contained a book inside. The book was called "The Lupus Book" (Wallace, D. J. MD.(1995). *The Lupus Book*. New York, Oxford: Oxford University Press)

My mother and I read the book but, it was very hard to understand because of all the medical terminology.

"Lupus is an autoimmune disease like my doctor had told us. A person with Lupus, has antibodies that attack a person's own tissue causing inflammation, instead of attacking bacteria and viruses.

When inflammation occurs, swelling develops, tissue destruction throughout the body occurs, and pain develops." **(Wallace, 4)**

I had an entire draw full of medications that I'd take every day. One of the medications I'd take called Prednisone, would swell me up. My face looked swollen, and three times bigger. I'd cry as I looked at myself in the mirror. I wasn't that skinny pretty looking girl anymore. I was bloated everywhere. My face looked like a chipmunk's face, and to me I looked obese, unattractive, and ugly. I felt ugly.

I had no more hopes about Bruno, or any other guy liking me because of my distorted self-image. There were many times I'd fall into a depression stage, and it would be very hard for me to snap out of it. My mother was always a great help to me. She'd tell me,

"Don't worry, Jennifer. This will soon be over with, and you'll be back to normal like you were before once everything is stable enough to take you off the medications."

Prednisone also made me very hungry, and because I hadn't taken this drug since I was a baby, I didn't know majority of my hunger was caused by it. Therefore, I couldn't control my appetite urges. I'd get up at three o'clock in the morning, and would make two big chourico sandwiches. I'd bring them to my bedroom and would eat them. My mother would wake up and start yelling at me.

"What are you doing eating at three o'clock in the morning?!"

"I'm hungry." I would respond.

My disease also had affected my brain somewhat. I would do stupid things like trying to make ice cream with cocoa power and milk, and then I'd put it in the freezer. When my mother would find it in the freezer, she'd yell at me for wasting all her milk. I also had a bike in the garage that was never assembled and when my parents weren't home one day, I put it under my bed. Why I did that? I have no clue. I think I was just determined to assemble it but didn't think of how I would if I didn't have the tools.

I was always very tired. That summer long, I watched television, ate and slept. That's all I did because, I didn't have much energy for anything else. All the medications I was taking just made me depressed and tired.

The Cytoxan treatments were very strong, and intense on me. I'd sit on a recliner in the Oncology ward for an hour while a small bag of straight medication would be given to me intravenously. After the treatment I would get very tired and weak. When I'd get home, all I wanted to do was sleep, and I'd go straight to bed. I had to do six treatments and by the time I got to the third, my hair started falling. When I'd comb it, some would stay on the comb. I kept telling my mother that I wasn't going to school bald, and that if I did get bald I was going to need a wig.

When school started again, I was still doing my treatments. It was very hard for me especially going to school the week after the treatment. On my last treatment I went to school right after because, it was the day before my math exam and my professor was going to give us a review. I felt so horrible, tired, and would dose off every once in a while in class. I was there but, at the same time I wasn't.

When I got home, I set the alarm clock for eight at night so I could study, and would sleep for three hours. When the alarm clock went off, I didn't want to get up for anything but, I did because I knew I had to study. As I studied, my eyes kept shutting. I was so tired. My body just wanted to collapse. On the day of my test, for some reason I got all nervous, uptight and couldn't concentrate. When I received the test back, I had tears in my eyes. I didn't even have one right answer, when I knew that I could've received a passing grade.

When winter came, I caught a terrible cold and because I didn't have much immunity, I got very sick. My doctor had me stay out of school for two weeks to recuperate and I did. However, when I went back to school I was so far behind. I had borrowed my friends' note-books and gathered all of the material to study over my week of Carnival vacation that following week. I had professors tell me that I could make up the exams when I was ready. They were so good to me, and tried to help me as much as they could.

Sunday morning while everyone was still in bed, my little sister Monique was up and was crying because she wanted someone to make her breakfast. My mother kept telling her to keep quiet, and that it was still early. I got up, and put on my sweater so I could make breakfast. As I walked down the corridor I felt myself getting hot, and felt like I was going to throw up. As I headed to the bath-room, I got dizzy and blacked out. My father heard loud banging as I hit the bathroom cabinets, and luckily he caught me in enough time before I wacked my head against the lavatory.

I could faintly hear my father shout out for my mother. She then came rushing into the bathroom. They took me to the emergency room, and I was admitted for a urinary tract infection. I spent my vacation in the hospital, and was so mad. I had made plans to go see some carnival dances with my cousin and her friend, and also study so I could catch up but it didn't turn out that way. I would cry so hard as the nurses kept puncturing me to find a vein for an IV.

"I don't deserve this! I don't deserve any of this! I deserve to be with my friends right now, and have fun watching Carnival dances! Not this! Why me! Why me!" I cried.

The nurse was unresponsive. I saw tears come to her eyes.

"I'm sorry." She replied.

I then felt bad. It wasn't her fault things weren't working out for me.

When I came home I felt much better but, I was getting stressed out because I hadn't studied anything and I knew that when I went back, there would be much more to study. I was overwhelmed. I felt like I had so many responsibilities on top of me, and wanted to resolve them all but, I just couldn't. I'd try to study but, I couldn't. I couldn't concentrate. I would get so uptight because, of the stress I had on top me that nothing would sink into my brain.

My blood work wasn't looking good, and my doctor was worried. At this point, I knew what I had to do. All of these stressors were putting my health into jeopardy, and the best solution to this was to drop out until I could finally recuperate fully.

I talked to my parents, they agreed, and so I quit school for that year so I could recuperate. However, I was home all day and was going insane. I didn't know what to do to get my mind off my health issues.

"Read a book." My mother would tell me.

That's just what I did. I read book after book, and that kept me entertained. I recuperated beautifully, and my blood work was great. Majority of my medications were dropped, and I felt more energetic and more like myself. I did exercise every day to get fit and in a couple of months, I was back to my normal figure. I was now determined to live life to the fullest, and make the best of each day.

I'd talk to my friends on the phone, and they'd tell me how much they missed me. They'd tell me that Bruno missed me too. I missed them all too but, I knew that quitting was the best thing for me to do at that point.

My parents started getting everything ready to sell the house so we could move back to America. They had put an ad on the newspaper, and in a couple of weeks we had a few offers. In October of 1999, we finally closed an agreement. A nurse and her fiancé bought the house. They seemed to be a very nice couple, and had told us that we could stay at the house until we departure.

I went and see my friends one last time before my departure and luckily, I caught my whole class outside waiting to get into the classroom. The first one my eyes searched for was Bruno. I missed him so much. I missed his smiles, his laugh, and his voice. As I looked at him, he smiled at me. To me that smile kind of felt as if he were saying,

"Jennifer, you're an amazing young woman."

He was wearing the jeans and shirt that I loved seeing him in with his cowboy belt. It was going to be hard for me to adjust not seeing him anymore because, I liked him so much.

Everyone was happy to see me. I told them I was going back to America because, there were better doctors there. My friend Sonia and Monica hung out with me that day. We went to the park in the city, and had lunch together. They gave me their addresses for us to always keep in touch, and I promised them I would.

I was determined to start a new life when I'd set foot in my homeland. I wanted to finish school, and wanted to attend college to become a Medical Laboratory Technician. I had plans once again, and hoped that God would keep me healthy for me to accomplish them. Life goes on, and so does my future.

8

Starting Over

When we arrived at Boston, Massachusetts, my grandparents started hollering,

"Jennifer! Monique!"

They were so happy to see us, and glad that we were back for good. We ran into their arms, and they loaded us up with kisses from cheek to cheek. I was glad to be back. I liked to live in the Azores too but, majority of my family was here. Besides, there were much more opportunities here, than in the Azores.

We were going to move into my great-grandmother's apartment house but, there had been a fire there. It was still in construction, and so we moved into my grandmother's house until the second floor was complete.

My great-grandmother was living there too for the same reason. My great-grandfather was no longer with us. He had passed away a year ago, and since he passed away my great-grandmother has suffered with a mild case of Dementia. Sometimes she wouldn't make any sense, and couldn't remember names of family members. However, she always remembered my name. I felt bad for her, and would sometimes talk to her and give her attention because that's what she needed. She needed someone to be patient with her, and show affection. My grandmother was always so busy, and didn't have much time to sit down and listen to her. At least now I can care for her like she cared for me when I was a child.

My parents registered me at Sunset High. I was placed in 12th grade, and didn't know anyone. Not even one of my Elementary or Middle school classmates was in my classes. I felt so lonely, and missed my friends in the Azores. I thought that after a few weeks I'd make some friends that I could hang out with but, it didn't turn out that way. It was amazing how much things had changed in four ages. High School felt more like the ghetto alley than a proper disciplined school. Majority of the girls had no pride and no shame on themselves flirting and giving themselves freely to any man. Their dress code was ridiculous. Most would dress like the ghetto, and some girls wore shirts that would reveal almost everything, and mini skirts that would show their butt when they would bend down. After school I'd see many guys and girls smoke pot, and all different types of drugs. I wasn't used to all of this, and neither did I want to.

I was always by myself because, I just wasn't that type of flirt that would pass on from guy to guy. Only when I truly liked a guy, was when I'd flirt. I wouldn't use it as a hobby. Maybe it was just this school. Maybe other schools weren't like this. I don't know but, I do know that this school was horrible.

Some girls would get jealous of me because, I'd get high test scores and they were failing. Why were they failing? They were failing because they wouldn't make the time to study, and instead would play around with their one night stand.

On my second semester, I meant this sweet girl from Bangladesh in my keyboarding class. She was a very nice person, and I started hanging out with her. Now I didn't feel so lonely any more, and was much happier.

In January we finally moved into my great-grandmother's apartment house. We moved to the second floor, and my great-grandmother moved to the first floor. The third floor was still incomplete, and no walls had been put up yet.

My grandmother didn't want her mother living alone because, of her mild case of Dementia but my great-grandmother was stubborn. She wanted to go back to her apartment. Because of her being stubborn, my grandmother, aunt and mother decided to pick days of the week that they could go check on her, and help her prepare meals.

As months passed by, her Dementia grew worse. Many times I'd catch her fighting to the television. She thought those people on television were real. Sometimes she'd put herself under the dinning room table and start crying because, she thought that there was a robber in the house. Sometimes she'd line the dining room chairs, and tell us that the children were sitting quietly.

On a very cold winter night, my great-grandmother walked all the way up to the third floor where there were no walls and slept there. In the morning one of the construction workers knocked at our door.

"Miranda, there's an old lady sleeping up stairs."

"Oh, my God! It's my grandmother." My mother replied, as she and my father ran up the stairs.

When my mother got up there, she noticed that my great-grandmother was all blue from the cold. My mother tried waking her up but, she was totally unconscious. My mother then called an ambulance.

Doctors gave us no hopes of her surviving because, her heart was very weak. When I went to see her at the intensive care unit, I started crying. She was hooked up to so many IV's, a heart monitor, and oxygen. I kind of reminded me of what I went through, and what I must have looked like when I was facing those worse moments in my life.

A few days later when my grandmother went and see her, my great-grandmother opened her eyes and then called out my grandmother's name.

"Beth." She said as her pulse got slower and slower until it reached to nothing. She passed away as my grandmother held her hand.

In the summer of 2001, I finally started working. I started of working as a cashier at a pharmacy close to home because, I didn't have my license yet. I was nineteen but, never had the chance to go for my license. Although I couldn't drive in order to enjoy my pay-check, it was nice to get a pay check every week. However, they started cutting hours. I needed the money to pay for driving school and a car and so, I had to look for something else.

It took me about a month but, I found a receiving job at Bradley's Fashion Boutique. It was a small retail store close to home that was convenient for me. We'd open shipment boxes, place price tags on all items, and security sensors on expensive merchandise. A month later they had a cashier position available, and so I put in a request to fill the position. They transferred me right on the spot.

I graduated from high school on my birthday, and boy I was so happy to be out of that school. My parents bought me roses, and made a little party for me at home.

Two weeks later I completed the sacrament of Confirmation, and my sister Monique completed the sacrament of Communion. My parents threw a big party for us at a local restaurant, and invited family and friends. It was fun, and we made seven hundred dollars all together. With that money, we bought a computer. We never had a computer before. This was our first.

A few days later, I received a letter of acceptance to Bristol Community College. Although I didn't get accepted into the Medical Laboratory Science program, I was still excited about starting college. It was a very competitive program many people would tell me. On the other hand, there were several prerequisites I needed to take for the program, and as a Liberal Arts student I was able to complete those which made me very happy.

My classes started on September of 2001. This school was very different from Sunset High! What a big difference! Everyone was so friendly, and willing to help anyone no matter what race or nationality a person was from. On my first semester, I made a couple of friends. I would hang out with a Portuguese group. Their names were Jack, Maria P., Maria S., and Isabel. They were so much fun to be with, and reminded me of my friends in the Azores.

Sometimes I would hang out with Jack alone. He was a very nice guy. Short like me, sweet, and made me laugh. After hanging out with him solo several times, I started liking him. I never thought I would like him that way but, it's as they say "You can't judge a book by its cover." I think because of all the attention he'd give me and his personality, I started to get interested in him.

Our speech class was the craziest class we had. On the first day, our teacher told us girls to never wear skirts in her class. Isabel, both Maria's, and I just looked at each other in wonder.

Well. Well. She had a point. I swear, my friends and I felt like we were in a class for mentally retarded children. Our teacher would make us lay down on the floor, and have us make weird gestures and sounds. Then she'd have us get up, and walk around the classroom doing those same gestures and sounds. I guess she figured, this was a way of us learning to not be ashamed if we look stupid in front of an audience. It was so embarrassing! Besides, the classroom door was open. I'd make every effort to stay away from the door.

One day she had us hold hands with a partner. Luckily, I had Jack. I was so nervous, and could feel myself getting hot. Inside I was praying that she would return us to our seats. Only after an entire minute, she sent us back to our seats. By that time, I was crisp.

As I got up for my routine school day, I gazed at the calender that was pinned onto my door. I noticed that it was already September 11 of 2001. It was two days before my math exam.

In the morning, I met up with my friends for class. Our teacher was talking about hijacking. I had no clue what he was talking about. After class I asked my friends.

"Hey! What was our teacher talking about?" I asked in wonder.

"You didn't see the news, today?" Jack was surprised.

"No. What happened?" I was curious.

"Terrorists hijacked two planes from Boston, and hit the Twin Towers!" Jack replied in panic.

"No! That can't be true!" I replied in shock.

"See for yourself." Jack replied as he pointed to the school monitor.

As I looked at the television, I felt as if the whole world had stopped.

"This can't be happening." I kept saying as I looked at the tragedy that was showing over and over again.

Many people started jumping off the building, when the first airplane had hit Tower One. Thick black smoke came gushing out of the building as the fire inside grew more and more intense.

About five later minutes later so they say, Tower Two gets hit by the second airplane and when this happened, both towers came down like two flat pancakes. Debris and toxic fumes came gushing through Manhattan with all it's force causing people to pass out. Manhattan was surrounded by a thick black cloud. On the streets there were tons of paramedics taking care of people. Some were those who had a chance to escape, and were severely burnt, or had suffered fractures due to concrete falling on top of them. They also helped those having difficulty breathing because of the toxic air that now consumed their city. It was a very depressing moment for all Americans. Nothing major like this has ever happened on American soil. To many it felt as if it were the end of the world.

After watching that horrifying news, I totally lost track of time and was heading to my math class. To my surprise, there was another class in there. I then thought that maybe my class was in a different classroom. I was going insane trying to find my class.

Before having a nervous breakdown, I asked a teacher if she could help me find my class. She asked me if I had my schedule, and so I pulled it out. After I looked at it, I took a glance at my watch and realized my math class was an hour later. I felt like a fool, and apologized to her.

"Oh. You don't have to apologize. Everyone is mixed up today because, of what happened to the World Trade Center." The teacher replied.

Next to my classroom, I sat down on a comfortable brown chair and started doing my homework. A minute later, this teacher with glasses and curly brown hair came out of her office, and started telling everyone to leave because the college was closing.

All state buildings closed around noon time. My mother picked me up, brought me home, and went back to work because her bank was only closing at one.

"We can't even be safe in our own country." My mother told me in despair as she drove me home.

When I arrived home, the phone started ringing. As I picked it up and held it against my ear, I could hear my grandmother from the Azores screaming and crying asking me if everyone was okay. I told her not to worry because, we were all fine. After that call I sought of got shook up. I still couldn't believe what was happening.

Later in the day I went to work. Unfortunately, they didn't close down Bradley's Fashion Boutique. As I entered the retail store, I could feel the damp and dead air hit my face. The atmosphere in there wasn't the same. It wasn't alive. It felt more like a darkness of sorrow. As I walked to the lounge, I heard the rumbling of the reporter coming from a small radio that was at the front registers.

I worked all evening, and would ask customers how they felt. Some wanted war against these terrorists, others gave no comment.

They were all so devastated. I was devastated too, and just wanted to go home and be with my family while watching the news that marked all Americans.

Around seven o'clock, my store manager gave everyone a candle, and we all went outside. Employees, and customers gathered outside while they held a lightened candle for a moment of silence. I witnessed many customers crying, and hugging each other. Hugging people, they didn't even know. In one way, this tragedy bought Americans together. It made Americans unite and bond to help the country, and to help each other overcome their grieving over this traumatic episode in their life. Many firefighters, and marines dedicated themselves to help find people that were caught in the rubble. Everyone helped in whatever way they could. Now the question was, what was the president going to do about this? Would there be war and revenge, or would there be peace? My answer to this was that only God knew what was yet to come.

After a while I realized that Jack had a girlfriend. I found out when I had noticed his engagement ring. The funny part of it all was that I worked with her, and we were friends. She was an associate in the sportswear department

However, one day Jack told me something that kept me wondering. I guess it's just a girl's thing that when a guy gives you a complement you take it for granted, especially if you like him.

As we were waiting for class to begin, he started staring at me. Then replied,

"Jennifer, there's something different about you today."

"What?" I smiled.

"Ah! I know! You're not wearing lipstick. You know Jennifer. You have such clear lips. Clearer than any other girl I've ever seen. May I give you a suggestion?"

"Ok?" I asked him in wonder.

"You look prettier without lipstick, or make up." He told me.

Jack and I were like brother and sister, and I wanted to keep it that way. I wasn't a boyfriend theft. I was a decent young lady, and didn't take men that were already taken.

My mother knew him from the pharmacy. Isn't that weird? Every guy I got attracted to, my mother would end up meeting him. I guess she was on the look out for me.

Jack was a good influence to me. He made me realize that I was much more than what I thought I was. He made me feel good about myself. I lacked self-esteem and with him I realized that even with the defect on my face, I was still beautiful.

On May 19 of 2002, my mother gave birth to another baby girl. That made us three ten years apart from each other. My middle sister was ten, and I was twenty years of age. She was such a cute bundle of joy. My parents named her Amanda Marie Wright. Unfortunately, I was always so busy between work, school and studying. Only when the summer came, was I able to spend more time with her. I would play with her, and make her laugh.

On the same year, I was accepted into the Medical Laboratory Science program. I didn't see Jack much anymore. However, I had made a bunch of new friends that were in my class. I would hang out with Jessica, Alana, Barbara, and Kim. They were fun and funny. We had our own little break room where every morning we'd brew a fresh pot of coffee, and take a breakfast break before class.

Now what do you think us girls would talk about and pass around the table?

Boys, of course. Alana would crack me up when she'd mention her crush to be her jungle of love. I never could keep my mouth shut, and neither could my friends. She'd make us laugh so much.

As they say, laughter begins joy into our hearts. I knew this program wasn't going to be easy but, with a bunch of happy girls school life turns out to be so much better. On the other hand, for me things seemed to turn out almost perfect. It seemed too good to be true. Someone special comes into my life. Someone who makes me feel like I have never felt before.

9

Falling in Love

This new guy came to work with us. He was a security guard from another store that had recently shutdown. He was short, plump, and had short black hair. He also seemed to be very quiet. However, he probably was because he didn't know anyone. One night when we were cleaning up the store, I went to accessories to clean and found myself stretching to reach the scarf hanger.

"Need some help there?" John asked me.

"Yeah. I think I could use some help." I smiled as I rested my heels to the ground.

This was how we met and ever since then, we turned out to be very good friends. More like brother and sister, I have to say. Whenever I was free of customers, and he was freely wandering through the store, he'd come up to my register and talk to me. He had such a handsome smile, and for some reason I felt so good when he smiled at me. I felt different. I don't know how to explain it but, there was something special about this man that I knew was going to affect my life, and affect the way I felt. I guess only time will tell.

A month had passed by since John started working with us but, for me it felt like several months. We talked quite often, and I was able to get to know him. He also was able to get to know me, and gave me a nickname. "Jenny Jen" he'd call me. I then started calling him "Johnny John," and we'd call each other by these nicknames left and right.

After a while some employees caught on, and started creating rumors about us. It's amazing how nasty people can get with such an innocent friendship. They started spreading the word that John liked me intimately, and that he was too much of a coward to tell me. When I found out, I felt awkward, confused, and uncomfortable around everyone in that place including John. I didn't know what to think because, I had never been put in a situation like this.

"Is it true that he likes me that way?" I kept asking myself.

One day when I went to the lay a way room to store some boxes, John some how spotted me and also went in.

"Have you heard about the things they've been saying about us?" John asked me.

"Yeah." I said as I bow my head down. I didn't know what else to say.

"None of it is true, Jenny. I just wanted you to know that. What about you, Jenny? Do you feel that way for me?" John asked me with a serious look on his face.

I didn't know what had happened to me that moment. I just froze, and couldn't think. The only thing I knew was that I wanted to get out of this rumor issue all together. I felt as if was a rotten egg in front of everyone. I couldn't help it. It was just the way I felt.

Suddenly words come out of my mouth. Words that I could've never imagined I would say. I truly didn't mean them. Why did I say them?

"I'd never like you that way." I replied.

After I finished, I couldn't believe what I had just said. I didn't mean it. Why did I say it? I was so mad at myself. I was just very frustrated because of certain people not leaving me alone about John liking me that way, which I knew wasn't true. I wasn't thinking straight. What I really wanted to tell him was that I liked him as a friend but, not that way. Not yet. Anyway.

I had apologized to him, and told him that this wasn't what I meant. He had taken my apology but, deep down inside I felt that he still held a little grudge on me because of that stupid remark. I hoped that within time he'd be able to forgive me.

After a few days, John and I were best buddies again, and it seemed like the rumors had quieted down. John told me he had a girlfriend, and that they've been together for a couple of years now. He also told me what he liked doing on his free time. He was a big concert fan, and also took the time to see the Patriots practice up in Boston. He also liked taking walks in the park.

After a while I realized we had so much in common. I loved going out and having fun, and loved taking walks around the park. I also loved to explore as much as I could of what this world had to offer, and so did he.

It seemed as time flew by, I started getting more and more interested in him. He was so full of life just like me. After several months, I became more and more attracted to him. I loved his smiles, his walk, and his talk. Sometimes I couldn't sleep at night because, I was too busy thinking about him laughing and giggling in the middle of the night. No matter how many times I'd tell myself that I couldn't like him that way, I couldn't but a barrier on my feelings. My feelings were stronger than my own conscience. My mind would tell me one thing, and my heart would tell me another.

Paula one of the associates, knew I was getting very interested in John and kept on telling me,

"John likes you, Jenny."

"He has a girlfriend." I kept on telling her.

"He doesn't care about her as much as he cares about you. Haven't you caught him looking at your legs when you wear skirts? I've seen him check out your butt, and your walk plenty of times." Paula would tell me.

"It can't be." I kept thinking but, deep down inside I wondered. He never really talked about his girlfriend.

"What if she's right?" I questioned myself over and over again. I wanted to believe Paula because, I liked him so much. She made it seem as if John was just too shy to tell me.

Paula just kept adding into the dough raising my hopes to a point that I just let myself go. I let the explosion of feelings take over my body, and at this point I had realized that I had truly fallen in love for the very first time. My heart was craving to be with him as often as I could, and when I wasn't with him I'd think about him every day. I was crazy about him. He had brought sunshine into my life, and made me happy.

Paula was right when she told me that he checked me out because the next time I wore a skirt, I caught him practically lying against the register counter in back of me staring at my legs. I then looked at him in the eye. He was about to laugh, and so I laughed with him. Ok. So he was attracted to me but, that didn't necessarily mean that he liked me that way. Did it?

When I had found out that Paula was lying to me about everything because she felt bad that I was 21 and didn't have a boyfriend yet, I was mad at her and stopped talking to her. She didn't help me. She just made things worse. Now I was in love, and it was hopeless. However, even if she didn't come into the picture, would I have still ended up liking Johnny this way? I think I would've but, I wouldn't have carried so much hope and would have stopped myself from letting my feelings take over.

On a Saturday evening I came to work, and was upset because of a fight I had with my father. John came up to me and asked me if I was ok.

"Yeah. I'm ok." I bow my head down.

"No. You're not ok. Tell me, Jenny Jen. You can trust in me." John came closer.

"I had a fight at home with my father, and he told me that I was never going to get married." That remark was bothering me so much but, Johnny made me feel so much better. He always had the right words, and the right way of saying things. He was always there for me. That was one of the reasons why I loved him so much.

"Jenny. That's not true. You're pretty, intelligent, and have a wonderful personality." John was mad at what my father had told me.

Beside him I felt loved, appreciated, and wanted. Wanted maybe just as a friend but, wanted.

As I woke up by sun that was beaming through my bedroom window on a beautiful Saturday morning, I suddenly remembered that I had to start work early.

"Oh, my God!" I shouted as I jumped out of the bed.

I only had fifteen minutes to get ready and as I was putting my pants on, I was also brushing my teeth at the same time. When I arrived at work, my manager questioned me,

"Jen. You're five minutes late. This is not like you. You're always early and perky."

"Well. I had a bad morning." I told her.

It was like a normal working Saturday where you never stopped ringing, and would get some obnoxious customers. When it finally died down, John came up to chit chat with me. A while ago he had asked me how to tell a girl she is hot in Portuguese, and so I told him. "Tu es fixe!" Today I asked him if he still remembered how to tell a girl that she is hot in Portuguese, and guess what he did?

As I was ringing out these two Portuguese young ladies, John starts to unbutton his shirt and starts giving me the eye and the two girls that were there as he said "Come on, baby!"

My face was red as a tomato, and I could feel butterflies racing through my body. As I was cashing out these two Portuguese girls, they started laughing. He was so funny. After they left, he looked at me with these luscious eyes and asked me if I liked it.

"It was good." I smiled.

I think he had done that to see how I would react. He always found a way to make me laugh, and smile. On the other hand, when he was unbuttoning his shirt, I just felt like grabbing him.

As the months flew by, I found it harder and harder to keep what I felt a secret. It seemed as if my feelings for him had surmounted as every month had passed by, and I just wanted to let it out, But how? I took me a while to figure it out but I came to the conclusion of writing him a letter, and this is what I wrote,

---

Dear John,   *12/20/03*

The first sentence is always hard for me but, I promise I'll be quick and straight forward. Remember along time ago when all those rumors went on, and when Paula told me those lies. Well, at the time I only liked you as a friend but, as time moved on things changed.

I started getting more and more attracted to you, until I finally realized that I had fallen in love for the very first time. I denied my feelings so many times thinking that this was probably just an obsession of mine but it didn't work because, this is far beyond an obsession. I love your walk, talk, and smile. You make me laugh, and I love your personality. You're such a wonderful and good-hearted person, Johnny. You deserve the best of what this world has to offer because, you are worth a million words.

Now that I know the truth, the only thing I want is for you to be happy with whom you love. I just want you to know that you are a good man Johnny, and should have someone that will treat you right. I will always be here with arms wide open whenever you need a friend or a sister to count on.

I want you and your girlfriend to have a Merry Christmas, and Johnny don't forget that you can always count on me!

Your friend,

Jennifer Wright

How do you think I gave it to him? There was only one person I could trust in that place, and that was my best friend Judy. I put the letter in a Christmas card, sealed it up, and gave it to Judy I as left. When I grabbed my stuff and was heading to the main exit, John came up to the door.

"Perfect timing" He said, as he finagled through my purse.

"I gave Judy something to give you." I smiled.

"Oh, yeah! I can't wait to see what it is." He smiled back.

I was only working weekends now because, school was getting quite intense. John usually didn't work on Friday's but, for some reason he was working this Friday. As I walked through the parking lot to the main entrance, I spotted his car.

"How am I going to face him?" I told myself as I began to get nervous.

As I headed to the bathroom, I saw him close by and took another route. I was so nervous because, I didn't know what to expect of him. When I arrived at my register, I had logged on and started cashing out my customers. After a while I felt a shadow behind me, and for some reason I knew it was John. After my last customer, I turned around and there was my Johnny John with his serious puppy eyes. He was making me so nervous. I tried keeping my cool and tried to avoid talking about the letter. Instead I asked him if he liked the Christmas card I gave him. However, he put me right on the spot. It seemed to me that the letter had great meaning to him.

"Jenny Jen, that letter meant a lot to me." John told me with such a serious expression.

I just smiled, and didn't know what to say. I was completely speechless. In one way, I was glad that I had made him feel good with my words. I guess it didn't hurt to be honest.

"Let's take a break, Jenny Jen so we can talk." John told me.

He told me he had a girlfriend, and it's been three years they've been together. He also told me that I was a very sweet person, and that I would find myself a good man.

Besides what he told me, he also mentioned that we should go out. This got me confused because, if I had a boyfriend that went out with another girl, I wouldn't like it one bit. Despite my opinion, I knew if he asked me I wouldn't be able to say no because I wanted to be with him. I loved him, and at this point I was just too fragile to do what was right.

On December 24, we worked and in between we had our Christmas party in the break room. There were all different types of food and pastry, and it turned out to be a fun day. Johnny had given me a Christmas card, and inside he had written a little message in regards to my letter. This is what he wrote,

---

Merry Christmas Jenny Jen!

I just wanted you to know that you're the kindest person at Bradley's Fashion Boutique. Don't let people tell you differently. More girls should be like you. Never let people get you upset, make you cry, or take advantage of you. I want you to always be happy because, you deserve to be happy. When someone gets you mad, just think of me. You're a special girl, smart, funny, and I love talking with you. Maybe we can hang out after the holiday's.

P.S. The letter meant a lot to me and again, thanks.

Your friend
John Arruda

No matter how many times I tried to forget and get rid of what I felt for him, my mission was never accomplished. All it took was one of John's smiles to light the flame. I tried to erase what I felt for him from my mind and heart but, it was unerasable. The only way I would be able to move on, was if I'd never see him again and I knew that wasn't going to happen anytime soon.

Time seemed to fly by. It was now June of 2004, and I was ready to graduate. I received my Associate's degree in Medical Laboratory Science with high honors, and was proud of it. I also had a job offer before graduation, and so that even turned out better. My friend Jessica and I were hired at a private lab in Brockton for second shifts, and we decided to car pool.

I had given my two-week notice to my manager at Bradley's Fashion Boutique, and was ready to start a new career and a new life. It was hard having to say my good byes to all my friends, especially John. I gave him a hug before I left and told him to keep in touch, and to keep smiling. I felt tears come to my eyes, and tried so hard to hold them back as I gave him my final smile.

A few days before I left Bradley's Boutique, I had found an Indian One Cent Penny in my cash draw. John always asked us if we had any because, he collected them. He once told me that it gave him memories of his grandfather that had recently passed away. When I had given it to him, he had thanked me and had told me that I was so sweet. That same day when he came to my register later in the day, he seemed depressed and had his head down.

"Where's that smile?" I asked him.

He then lifted his head and gave me such a handsome smile. I could tell that I had triggered his heart, and made him feel better. On the other hand, I felt so good. It was as if I breathed his smile within my heart.

Words can't explain or express how much I liked him.

John was the: *Joy*

> *Of my*
> *Heart and*
> *Never ending*

Only God, and I knew what was inside my heart.

10

A New Career

I started training 1st shifts as a Medical Laboratory Technician, at a U.S. Laboratory in Brockton right after graduation, and enjoyed working there. However, my job was strictly lab tech work. There was no patient contact whatsoever. We were just confined in this private lab with no contact to the outside world. I knew this was going to be a great challenge for me because, I loved being around people.

Besides this downfall, I liked the job it's self. I felt like a scientist, as I tried figuring out each patient's health issue by analyzing their blood and urine specimens. I had to operate a lot of analyzers most of the time but, for me my favorite part of my job description was looking through the microscope at blood smears to detect abnormal cells in the blood, and urine slides to detect for infection. I mostly liked this part of my job because, I was able to think and use my judgement. Sometimes it could be frustrating when I couldn't differentiate certain cells but, I still loved it. Besides, our lab took care of almost all nursing homes in Massachusetts and it was very rare to see normal results.

I took my job seriously because, any mistake could end up being life threatening to a patient. This job was important to our community because without lab results doctors wouldn't be able to truly and accurately diagnose a patient, and you know this would make me think,

"Why do nurses get all the big bucks, and we don't?! We're like scientists. We also have a plenty of responsibility on our shoulders. Doesn't the government recognize that?"

My parents for a moment were deciding to move to Florida. They didn't know what they wanted. Why couldn't they just stay put, and be happy where they were?

"If you guys are serious about going down there to live, go ahead but I'm not going." I told my mother.

"Why not, Jennifer? We would be much closer to Disney World." My mother insisted.

"I don't care! Besides, I've made so many friends here and all my doctors are here. I'm not going and that's final." I replied.

After a while my parents stopped talking about moving. I guess they didn't want to move without me. Besides all the reasons I stated to my mother, there was also another reason to that as well. I never told my parents that I liked someone. They had no clue I liked John, and went by Bradley's Boutique almost every week to see him after work. I couldn't help myself. I missed him so much. I just had to see that handsome smile of his.

Many times I'd catch him in his little security cubicle watching the security monitors, and would sporadically pop in. I always enjoyed every second I was with him, and would come home feeling so good and so happy. He always made me feel good, just by his smiles and his words. When I was with him, I always lost track of time. Sometimes when I'd come home, my mother would ask me where I had been. I'd tell her that I had gone by Bradley's Boutique and see my friends. I never told her the exact truth because, I was afraid she'd get mad at me. Sometimes I thought my parents were just too hard on me. I was twenty-two now and wasn't a child anymore. I was able to make my own decisions.

I'd also talk with John online, and would sometimes spend hours talking with him. I remember one particular day when he asked me to go by Bradley's Boutique, and I was so happy to know that he wanted to see me that I picked out the sexiest clothing I had in my wardrobe to go see him. He was so sentimental that day for some reason. I loved that serious face! It made me crave him more and more. That day he told me that he always wanted to see me happy, and I told him the same and smiled back. It seemed like every time I went and see him, the more I wanted him. Sometimes I'd stop and think to myself,

"Jennifer. What are you doing? Your just sinking yourself deeper into the pie, and the deeper you sink the harder it will get for you to get out and move on. Besides, he has a girlfriend and doesn't like you that way. If he did, he would've already told you."

My mind knew this but, my heart was a different story. I guess I just never wanted to let go of all the hope I carried with me even knowing that my chances were very minimal. It was so easy to fall in love but, so hard to fall out of love.

Every week I'd say to myself,

"This will be the last day I see him."

However, it never lasted beyond two weeks.

"What am I going to do?" I'd tell myself.

By the end of the summer, my parish always had a Holy Ghost feast. My parents, grandparents, and I went on one of the feast nights. There was music playing, lots of games to play, and food to munch on. While I was just standing there, I spotted Scotty! Remember? He was my defender in Elementary school, and had told me he wanted to marry me.

When he saw me, he began to approach me. I got so nervous. Was he going keep his promise? When he finally got close to me, he asked,

"Do you know who I am?"

"Yes. You're Scott. I went to school with you." I told him.

I was nervous about what he was going to ask me next. Was he going to ask me out? Nope. That wasn't it. He asked me how I was doing.

"I'm doing fine. How about you?" I asked

"I'm ok. Many times I usually see you walk alone at Bristol Community College. What are you taking?" Scott asked.

"I was in a Medical Laboratory Science program, and graduated this year. I'm now working at U.S. Laboratory. What about you?" I asked

"I'm studying Science Engineering. Later, I'm transferring to University of Massachusetts Dartmouth." He told me.

His friends then came up to him and started talking to him, and that's how the conservation ended. I meant Scott again. I wonder if later down the road when we're both ready, we meet again and stay together. I only like him as a friend but, only God knows who's meant for me, and who will make me happy for the rest of my life.

As soon as I started 2nd shifts at work, I was beginning to dislike my job. There was no 3rd shift, and the nights turned out to be extremely long. Every time I was ready to leave, STAT's would come in and I'd have to stay to get them done. I'd end up working 12 hour shifts, and only getting five hours of sleep every day. I had no life. My life was just sleep and work, and that wasn't what I wanted.

After about two weeks it caught up to me, and my blood work was not looking good. I told my doctor about my job, and he had advised me to find something that would be less stressful for the time being because, stress could cause my sickness to return.

He ended up ordering a 24hr urine and some blood work, and when the results came back, he realized my sickness had already flared up and triggered my kidney's. I ended up quitting my job and went back to Bradley's Boutique where it was less stressful, and besides I was close to my Johnny John. My doctor referred me to a

Nephrologist and from that day on, I knew things were going to get complicated.

I was very depressed and very angry.

"Why does everything have to fall on me?" I 'd tell myself.

That day after I left the doctor's office, I drove to Buttonwood Park and took a walk around the park. I just didn't want to be bothered. I wanted to think about other things, and forget about what the doctor had told me. I knew that thinking of John was my best remedy, and that's how I sent my afternoon in the park. Just thinking about him, and picturing his smile in my mind and in my heart, made me feel so much better.

That night I talked with him on the internet. He was depressed too. He told me he was having problems at work, and with his girlfriend. I was sad to hear that he was sad, on top of what I was dealing with. I told him that things would get better. I just wanted to cheer him up.

However, what I really wanted to do was be along side of him and comfort him. I wanted to hug him and tell him personally that everything would be ok. The following day, I wore a shirt to spike up John's smile. As I started talking to Gary, John suddenly popped in and Gary tried covering his eyes.

"You can't see the way Jenny is dressed." Gary told him.

I had jeans on and a shirt that had this saying in big letters,

"I saw what you did! I'm in love!"

I started laughing. When Gary finally let Johnny look at me, Johnny seemed to get all bubbly when he read what was on my shirt. He knew I liked him. I guess he just never felt that way for me. The odd thing was that we got along so well, and he seemed to be attracted to me too. Maybe that's the reason why I carried so much hope.

That day I told John about my sickness and how it flares up. He was so supportive and understanding. Sometimes he helped and understood me more than my own parents did. John and I were always there for each other.

I was nervous when I entered my Nephrologist's office. She seemed very nice, and had set up a renal biopsy for me. When the results came back that same day I had done the biopsy, that night I received a phone call from my doctor.

"Jennifer, your kidneys are very inflamed. I want you to report to the hospital tomorrow morning immediately, to start treating you which intravenous corticosteroids." My doctor told me in panic.

After I hung up the phone, I began to cry. My mother then walked in, and asked me what the doctor had told me.

"I have to go to the hospital first thing in the morning tomorrow because, my kidneys are very inflamed." I cried.

"At least your kidney's are working, Jennifer. Come here." My mother replied, as she wrapped her arms around me.

"I'm just afraid that I'm going to have another major flare like last time, mom. It may be triggering my kidneys, and then move onto my heart and lungs." I cried.

"I don't want to face death again, mom." I wept.

While I was in the hospital, my doctor came and visit me.

"How are you doing, Jennifer?" She asked.

"I'm ok." I told her.

"Jennifer. I don't know what your plans are for the future but, at this point you will have to make a decision."She told me.

"What do you mean?" I said in worry.

"You are in need for a six-month trial of Cyclophosphamide, which is a form of chemotherapy, and this treatment may completely destroy your reproductive system."

"So this means that I will never be able to have any children?" I told her as I let out painful cries.

"This may be the case, Jennifer. There is a medication that I might be able to put you on by getting approval from your gynecologist to preserve your ovaries if you intend to have children in the future. However, that's only if she finds it safe for you." The doctor explained.

"Yes, I would like that." I replied.

"This chemotherapy will quiet your sickness again and heal your kidneys. We can't afford to try anything else at this moment because, you may end up with kidney failure." She told me.

After she left the room, I began to cry.

"What if it's not safe for me to take that medication while I'm having chemotherapy treatments?" I'd say to myself.

"I'll never feel woman enough to any man if I'm not fertile. That was always a part of my dream." I cried as I wrapped the hospital blanket around me.

Later that day, my best friend Judy came and see me. She brought me so many things. I couldn't believe it. She had bought me a CD player that also had a radio, a CD, a nice soft teddy bear for me to hug when I was depressed, and lots of candy. She was such a sweet and giving person, and cheered me up all the time. I told her what the doctor had told me, and about my possibly of never having children. As I cried, she saw the agony and pain that were inside of me, and cried along with me. She was more then just a best friend. She was like a sister to me. After she left, I felt better.

When I came home after three days in the hospital, I talked with John online.

"Don't worry, Jenny Jen. You'll get through all of this, sweetheart." He wrote me.

John was one of the most patient and understanding guys I've meant. I could tell when he would listen attentively to a person and when he didn't, and to me it seemed that everything I would tell him would always be of interest to him. He was one special man, and was my happiness.

A few days later, I went by Bradley's fashion Boutique to see my friends. They gave me this big Get Well card with everyone's name on it. That was so sweet of them. Everyone was happy to see me, and gave me their comfort and support. I felt so loved.

After a while, I saw my Johnny. He was waiting patiently as always for me to approach him to talk. As I approached him, he told me,

"Jenny Jen. You're such a brave girl. Come here! Talk to me."

After I had heard his voice, I was already feeling much better. I had told him what was going to happen next, and he told me he'd always be there for me anytime I needed his comfort and support.

Before I left, I asked him for a hug. This hug was different from the last one. There were feelings to it. It felt as if he were glad that he didn't lose me. I didn't want to let go. I felt so loved and protected in his arms. At that moment I deep down inside wanted to say those three words but, I knew it was inappropriate. Instead I told him,

"Thank you, John. I missed you."

When I was ready to leave after talking to some other friends, I passed by John's security cubicle to say goodbye and there he was sitting on the floor with his legs crossed. I was going to just say goodbye but, he gave me a look as if he were telling me,

"Don't leave just yet, Jenny Jen."

So, I ended up staying and talked with him for a while. He told me stories to make me laugh and smile again. He wanted to see me happy like I was before.

After when I had gone home, I felt so much better. That night I just wanted pour out what I felt about all of this that was happening, and so I sat down and wrote in my diary.

Dear Diary,   *09/20/04*

Life is just not fair especially for those who are good, and try to make the world a better place. It seems like the good suffer for the rotten ones out there. I've suffered all my life since I was born with a Hemangioma, and now with a much more devastating case called Systemic Lupus since I turned seventeen. Right now I'm on medication to help certain areas and on the other end, it ends up hurting other areas. My body image is so distorted that I don't even dare to look in the mirror most of the time, and when I do I feel like crying. I'm on high dosages of Prednisone, and this drug is the main cause for my swelling and chipmunk face. I feel so ugly!

I keep praying to the Lord, and ask Him to put this disease in remission forever, and told Him that I'd take care of myself. I hope He's listening. I will not do any more crazy diets. I'll be sure to wear sun screen at all times when it's sunny, and not work 60 hours a week like I was doing. I'm just that type of person who is always waiting for a challenge but, I learned that I can't be a superwoman anymore. My body is just not fit for it

Why did God give me such a worthless body, when my insides don't match it? Why did I get the challenge of defeating sickness, and not just succeed in anything I want to? Why me? I want to do so much in this world, and it seems like I get stopped all the time with health problems.

Why can't I have a normal life like everyone else? There are so many things I want to accomplish in this world. All I'm asking you Lord, is to give me a chance.

I want to be one of the many women to make a difference here on earth. I want to be recognized as a strong woman and a role model to everyone, especially those who suffer as well. I want to show the world that no illness or disease will ever stop me from accomplishing my dreams in life and that no matter how hard my road gets, I'll keep on dragging my feet and never look back.

I have great expectations. I'm looking forward to becoming a doctor or nurse practitioner someday.

However, I know I can't do it alone. I need God to give me a chance to live a normal life, and need the support of my family and friends, to help me along the way because, without them I wouldn't have made it this far. They make a big difference in my life.

Sincerely,

Jennifer Wright

My parents bought a house in Swansea. It was a very nice, and big house with an in ground pool in the back. What really made me happy was that I was able to have my own room. I turned my room into a Paris village, with all sorts of Paris accessories. I loved it! Besides, the neighborhood was very quiet and peaceful.

My first chemotherapy treatment went ok. It was a six-hour treatment and for me to not get bored, I had brought my Cd's and Cd player so I could listen to music while I did the treatment. The first song I listened to was "White Flag" by "Dido." It reminded me of John. It reminded me of him because, one night while I was warming up my car, I had this song blaring and the next day when John saw me, he told me he heard the song playing from my car and, told me that this was one of his favorite songs. I spent my afternoon at the Oncology ward listening to music, and thinking of my Johnny John. It helped me face and defeat the weakness and tiredness that were consuming my body due to the treatment.

When I'd finished the treatment, I'd leave the Oncology ward very weak and tired. I couldn't stand for long periods of time, and would doze off every once in a while. Although I was only taking a low dosage, I was a small person and just this small dosage turned out to be a lot for my body to handle. When my father brought me home, I rested in bed and watched television. In a few minutes I was sound asleep. My doctor had warned me to be extra careful for infection because, the chemotherapy lowers my resistance. Other than that, I was doing ok and had three days to rest before I had to go back to work.

Thursday I went back to work after my therapy session. I was still feeling a bit weak, but glad to be back at work. I took one step at a time and when I'd get tired, I'd take a break. My managers were very supportive and understanding. They kept telling me,

"Jen. If it's too much for you just let us know."

That same day I was singing a "Tina Turner" song that was playing on the radio as I was putting sensors on some jackets next to the registers. After a while I started getting a little loud and told myself,

"Gee, I better stop singing or else people are going to think I'm some kind of freak."

After I stopped singing, John came down the stairs singing the same song. He made my smile. He always made me smile, and feel better. He was like a brother to me, and I was so thankful for that because I didn't know how I would've handled this on my own. My parents tried to understand what I was facing but, they never understood what I felt like. Besides, they never had much time to sit down and talk with me but, John did. He was patient and was always there for me. He had made a great difference, and helped me when I was in great needs of emotional and psychological support. I will always carry his goodness within my heart, no matter what life brings me. He'll always have a place in my heart.

When he came down the stairs and approached me, he gave me a hug.

"How's my Jenny Jen doing?" He asked.

It felt so good to know he cared. Besides, he knew when I wasn't feeling good. I didn't even have to tell him. He could see it in my eyes. At that moment I just wanted to cuddle in his arms and feel his warmth and his heartbeat. I loved him so much, and he showing me he cared made me love him even more.

On November 13 of 2004, my grandparents and I went to see "Dolly Parton" sing live at the Mohegan Sun. I wasn't a great fan but, I still enjoyed it. After the concert, we gambled for a little while. I wasn't too fond about giving away my money to a slot machine but, I gave up ten dollars.

Before we left, I bought two pictures of "Dolly Parton" that had her autograph stamped on it.

"I have to get one for John. I know he will like it, and again I'll make him happy." I thought to myself.

Sunday, as I left the break room with the envelope that contained the picture, I encountered John on my way to the elevator.

"Hey, Jenny Jen!" He smiled.

"Hey! I've got something for you." I smiled back.

"Jen, you're always full of surprises. I wonder what you're going to surprise me with now." His smile extended from cheek to cheek.

When he pulled out the picture, he was very surprised!

"This is nice Jenny Jen but, why do you take your time to surprise me with such good things?" He told me with such a serious expression.

Maybe no girl he's ever dated ever took the time to impress him as much as I did. Maybe not even his girlfriend. He knew I liked him but, maybe he never experienced this type of love where the girl tries so hard to make him happy and compensate for what he has given her. Words can't explain how much I loved and cared about him. If he were my boyfriend, I'd make sure he'd be happy and would have everything he wanted, and most of all I'd love him to death. But what was I talking about? I was only the girl next door. I'd never be a part of him because, he loved someone else.

"Because I wanted to." I told him.

What I really wanted to say was,

"Because I love you."

However, that wasn't my line to say. It was his girlfriend's line. Not mine. At the registers he thanked me again, and told me that no other girl has even done that for him before. I felt special. Luis other hand turned around and said,

"She's in love."

Johnny was very serious. He knew it was true. I had shown him in many different ways. I could tell I had triggered his heart once more.

After my fourth treatment, my hair started falling. Luckily, I didn't lose much up until I finished my treatments. After my treatments were over with, my doctor put me on an immunosuppressant called Celcept. She told me that it would regulate my immune system, and keep my disease in remission. Hopefully it would for good. I was very happy but you know, some medications work on some people and not on others.

Sometimes I'd get so desperate for a change in my life because, my life seemed the same every year. I was either working myself out between work and school, or working myself out by beating my disease. This wasn't the lifestyle I wanted. In addition, being in love just made things worse because I was always dying for a change, and was always so anxious to find that Mr. Right who could love me the way I loved John. There were moments in my life when I was with John that I just felt like letting my feelings pour out. I had so much to offer to that one special man who was meant for me, and to me Johnny was the one whom I wanted it to be so badly. It was always so hard for me to hold back everything I truly wanted to give him.

I just wanted a change that would make me happy, and never bore me for the rest of my life. I knew that being happily married and having my own family would never bore me out, and would make me happy till the day I die. Continuing school didn't matter

as much to me as getting married and having a family. This was all
I've ever wanted.

Dear Diary,   *09/10/05*

*I'm so sick and tired of the same boring, and lonely life I have. I
need to be loved. I need lots of love. I need some special man to
wrap his arms around me, and tell me that I was the best thing
that has ever happened in his life. Sometimes I break down and
cry because, all I want is to have a normal life. I want to get married and have kids. I want to be the best wife and mother I could
be for that special someone whom I await for so anxiously. However, life never leads me to my dreams because I always get
hammered down by sickness one way or another. I'm sick of
fighting, and only being happy for little spurts here and there in
my life. When is this going to end?! I feeling lonely just makes
me feel worse, and at certain points when I was doing my chemotherapy, and felt so horrible, I'd ask myself,*

*"Why should I even exist if all I do is suffer, and on top of it all
I'm lonely and don't have anyone to comfort me and love me?"*

*I just want to be happy! Happy for the rest of my life. I want to
have reasons to live for. If Johnny wasn't in my life, I don't know
what I'd do. He is one of the reasons why I want to live. He
understood how I felt, and was there for me as a brother. He was
a gift God sent my way because, God knew that John was going
to help me get through all my problems during my treatments.*

*When will be the day when I'm squeezed in between some spe-
cial man's strong arms, and be kissed to death for him loving me
for whom I am? When will be the day that I'm asked in marriage,
and experience tears of joy come my eyes? When will be the day
that I come walking down that church aisle with my wedding
dress shining like Cinderella? When will be the day that I'm married and snuggled up in bed with my husband wrapped around*

me giving me all his body heat, and all his sweet and tender love?

When will be the day that I become a mother for the very first time to a healthy baby boy or girl that my husband and I created with so much love? When will be the day that the sun finally shines my way and fulfills my dreams? Lord. I need your help! Help me find that prince that awaits me. I know that patience is a virtue but, I've been waiting for so long.

Sincerely,

Jennifer Wright

I hadn't seen John for two weeks because, he was working at another site. When I saw him, it seemed like he had brought the sunshine with him, and placed it right back into my heart.

He told me he hated the fact that he didn't see me much, and wanted to spend more time with me.

"Why don't we go out for lunch or dinner one of these days? What do you say?" John asked me.

He was serious about it. I knew he wasn't just playing around with me, and knew he really wanted to go out with me. I knew the right answer was,

"No, you have a girlfriend and that's just not right."

However, nothing could convince my heart to say that. All it took was his smile to think yes and nothing else.

"Yeah. I'd like that." I smiled back.

I knew John was only going out with me as a friend because he never really saw me much anymore but if his girlfriend found out, I don't think she'd be too happy. Besides, it's a small world.

"It will only be this once." I'd tell myself.

When it was five o'clock, he called me. I practically ran to the phone so my mother, father, or sister wouldn't pick it up. For the first time he called me instead of me calling him. He sounded like he was nervous, and so was I. We ended up meeting at Friendly's and in the beginning, I was very nervous. This was the first time I had ever gone out with a guy before by my lonesome. It felt like my first date. I knew that I could trust in him because, he was my friend and had always been like a brother to me. As we dined, I felt like my nervousness had slipped away and comfort had replaced it. We talked about our families, dreams, and work of course. Johnny had told me that his father was a diabetic, and that he had to have a kidney transplant when Johnny was a child. He also told me that his mother was a hard worker who sacrificed to pay the bills since she was the only one working. Johnny told me that even with the crappy pay he'd make at Bradley's Boutique, he'd help his parents as much as he could. I was very proud of him. He was a caring and loving person, just like me.

That night he told me he had a wonderful time, and I had told him the same. This had turned out to be one of the happiest days of my life.

Just being with him felt so good, and meant so much to me. He was the boy who made my heart race, and made my insides melt.

11

Feelings

Johnny's birthday was on April 12 and I wanted to throw him a big party because, I wanted to show him how much I cared about him. I had him invite whomever he wanted, and took care of the rest. I bought him a birthday card, and went to Bradley's Boutique to have everyone sign it. Sometimes he'd get suspicious, and come after me to see what I was doing. I'd try to hide it and for a moment, he almost caught me. He had come up to me, and as I was in front of the counter draw, I slid it inside.

"Can I see if there's gum in there?" He asked me as he smiled.

"You can't go in there." I laughed.

"So it's restricted. I wonder why?" He had a smirk on his face.

While he turned around, I quickly took the card out and hid it somewhere else.

"Ok. It's not restricted any more." I told him

When he opened the draw, he looked around to see if he saw anything as he also looked for some gum. That same day before I left, I don't know what happened to me but when I looked at him, I started getting these tremendous cravings. Cravings to hug him and kiss those sweet lips of his. I then turned away. I couldn't love him this way, and it seemed like I couldn't stop myself. Besides, I didn't know how to put an end to all of this. This was my first time. I had never felt this way in my entire life, and I guess I just didn't want to let go of what made me so happy.

I ordered him a cake that had a decor of the Boston Red Sox, and also bought him two gifts. One he wanted, and the other was a funny one to make him laugh. On his birthday early that morning, I went and give him the card while they were all having their Pre-Conference meeting. He gave me these serious eyes and thanked me. I could tell that I had triggered this man's heart once more. After I gave him the card, I took a walk around the store to check out some spring clothes. Right before I left, I saw him talking with Gary and told them to have a good day. John then turned around and told me thanks once again with such serious puppy eyes. When I went to say you're always welcome, I got those craves again and felt tears come to my eyes because I knew he could never love me the way I loved him.

"See you at five o'clock." I told him as I left.

"Jennifer. Wait. Come here. I want to give you a hug." John told me as he smiled.

He knew how I was feeling. He could see it in my eyes. When he hugged me, I felt so relieved and so comfortable as I let my feelings shed onto him.

"Thank you." I told him as I looked at him and smiled.

We had gone to Olive Garden, and celebrate his birthday party there. It was nice to talk with some of my friends from Bradley's Boutique out of work for a change. After we ate, I ordered the waiter to bring out the cake. I had my camera ready, and in a few seconds all the waiters came marching out with the cake singing happy birthday. I stared so happily at his serious speechless face as the candle flames danced back and forth. Once again, I had triggered his heart.

"Blow out your candles." I told him with a bright smile.

I took pictures of him blowing out his candles, and also took pictures of my friends. Then I asked one of my friends to take a picture of John and I together. After she had taken the picture, she had told us that we looked nice together.

After everyone left besides Eugene, I knew I had to leave soon too. Before I left, there was a moment when John and I were alone. I glanced at his handsome face, and boy at that moment I wanted to be his girl. I wanted to be wrapped up in his arms and wanted to kiss him.

"Jenny Jen, tell me what you want. I'll give you anything you want. Just ask me. You've done so much for me." He told me with a serious expression.

I knew what I wanted but, I knew it would never come true. I felt my eyes getting heavy, and couldn't respond to his question.

"What are you thinking, Jen? Come on. Tell me now, and not later down the road." John told me.

"Is it good thoughts?" He asked.

I nodded in a yes gesture, and then changed the conversation. Even if I told him that what I wanted was to be with him for the rest of my life, it wouldn't have changed anything! He didn't love me that way. Why should I even bother? He knew I liked him. I had shown him in various ways, and yet nothing changed and nothing will change because, I'm only a friend and nothing else but a friend. That night when I arrived home, I sat by my computer and wrote in my diary.

Dear Diary,   *4/12/05*

I know I have to rid myself of these feelings I have for him but, it's just been so hard. There are moments when I feel that I wouldn't be able to live if I never saw him again. It's just so hard on me. Every time I look at John, I see my happiness, and my love that I can't retrieve. What am I going to do with all these feelings I've consumed for so long? I just end up getting dispar-

ate to find that Mr. Right who will love me in return. However, in my heart I've always wanted it to be Johnny since the first day I had realized that I was in love.

Sincerely,

Jennifer Wright

In June of 2005, I was hired for a Medical Laboratory position at a Fall River walk-in clinic. It was convenient, and close to home but, the volume there was much lesser than the volume we had at US Laboratory. Sometimes I would get bored but, in the long run it was better for me because I had less stress on my shoulders. I worked with a bunch of funny ladies who made me laugh constantly. They always had funny jokes to make me laugh. When I first meant our courier named Stephen, I was kind of timid because he was so tall. However, when I was able to open up with him, I realized he was a very sweet, and soft-spoken man. I don't even think he'd hurt a fly. Beth. S, and Beth. O. always kept me on my toes, and included me to the conversations. Muff on the other hand, would make me scared when she trained me because she was so tall, and would move so fast that if I was in back if her shadowing, she'd crush me if she so happened to take a step back. I always had to extend my neck twice as hard to look at her but, she was a very nice person.

Dottie May was short like me, and she was very sweet too. Luis my manager, was mostly busy in his office and it took me a while to actually open up with him because, I never knew when was a good time to talk with him. When I did get to know him, he was like a second father to me. Every day when I'd come in and stop by his office to say Good Morning, he'd smile and ask me how I was doing. I'd ask him the same and always smiled back.

My life seemed to be heading in the right direction now. I had a job close to home in my field of study, and had finally left Bradley's Fashion Boutique for good but there was something thing missing. My prince was missing. It's true that I was happy with what I had but, I was desperate to find that special man who could love me.

A couple of weeks later, Johnny had called me at work.

"Hey, honey. Would you like to go out after work?" He asked me.

Now what do you think I said? What would you answer to his question? You know me more than anyone else.

"I'd love to." I told him as I smiled.

My bad! Didn't I learn my lesson about not going out with someone who was committed to someone else?! What was wrong with me? It wasn't about the whole issue of going out as a friend. It was about me liking him more than just a friend. When I'd go out with him I'd get so attached to him, and for some reason I was always waiting for that magic I've always dreamed of between him and I.

I guess I was just a foolish girl. I couldn't help it. He sounded so sweet on the phone, and called me honey. I just couldn't say no as an answer. As we waited for seats, my mother called me on my cell phone. She never knew that I had gone out with John these two times. I was always afraid to tell her because, I knew she was going to break through all of this. Luckily, she had called to find out what time I was going to be home. I was glad that this was all she asked because I didn't like to lie, especially to my mother.

It turned out to be one of the best days of my life once again. We laughed, and smiled as we talked about our dreams, family and concerns. He always made the day so special for me. Every time we went out, I'd get all happy dressing up to impress him. Sometimes I had to lower my tone because, my parents would get suspicious. At least this second time I wasn't nervous. I was comfortable beside him, and didn't want leave! When we left, I asked him if he could give me a ride to my car because my car was at a different parking lot, and so he took me. I have to admit that I was nervous when I was all by myself with him in his car but, it felt so good. Then we said good night and when I looked deep within his eyes, my poor heart started melting. That night I couldn't sleep! I was always tossing and turning thinking about him, and laughing in the middle of the night.

When I woke up the next day, I felt so rested and so happy! Boy, just going out with him made me feel so good. I couldn't imagine how I would feel if we were girlfriend and boyfriend! I think by then my life would have been complete, and I'd be one of the happiest girls on this earth but, what was I talking about! He had a girlfriend and besides, he'd probably never like me that way.

My parents had gone to Terceira for one week. I couldn't go because I had just started working thirty-two hours at Prima Care, and hesitated to ask for the time off. I ended up having the house to myself for one week. It felt good to be the owner of the house for that week. No parents to bother me, and I could do things the way I wanted. My mother alerted me that just because they weren't home, she still wanted me to obey my curfew and that day of their departure when I got home, there was a big letter for me and it mainly said,

"Please keep your curfew because, God is watching you."

Can you believe that?! She wanted to put God against me, if I didn't obey her orders. She knew how I was. I always tried my very best to obey the Lord and do the right thing.

Before they had gone, many of my friends had mentioned going out that week since I would be by my lonesome but, it turned out that none of them got in touch with me. Besides, I was always working and would end up getting tired by the end of the day. So I guess I could say I did obey my curfew. Even if I didn't, she would find out because my grandmother would call me constantly to check up on me. One day I worked extra hours, and when I got home there were fifty million messages!

"Jen? Jen? Where are you Jen? Please call me Jen! I'm worried about you Jen!"

She was worse than my mother! I was an adult now, and knew how to take care of myself! Besides, if something happened I would've called her. Even my godfather told her to stop worrying because, I was an adult and knew how to take care of myself. That day I called her, and she was all panicked.

"Where were you? I was worried about you?!"

"I ended up working extra hours."

"Well, you could have at least called me and warned me."

I really couldn't do things my way but, at least I was able to have the house to myself. If it was for me, I'd go out every day after work. Either take a ride up to Buttonwood Park or go watch a movie and hang out at the mall. Shopping, entertainment, and nature were the things I loved most.

Before my parents arrived home, I cleaned the house, and did the laundry. When they came home, they were happy to see me and had told me how my grandmother out there was a pain in the neck. She would always ask them where they were going and if they arrived home a little late, she'd be praying to the saints.

My mother got so heated up one day and told my grandmother,

"There is no need for you to be worried about us because, we're already grownups. Now I'm the one that should be worried because, I left a very sick daughter by herself in order to come here!"

They had shown me the pictures they took. It was nice to see my grandparents, aunt, and cousins again. However, my grandmother looked older and drained out. She over did herself! She cleaned that huge house all by herself and when I talk about cleaning, I mean cleaning down to detail for example, she'd scrub the floors and wash the windows every week. She was a diabetic and was wearing herself out too much. This wasn't good for her.

In July, my mother and I went for our Gynecology appointments. My mother also went for a mammography test and after our appointments when we were about to leave, a medical assistant from the mammography clinic next door called my mother. She told her she had to go to Charlton Memorial Hospital for an ultrasound because, they had found something. My mother was already getting nervous, and had tears coming down her eyes. I tried holding myself together so I wouldn't burst out in tears myself. I kept telling her that maybe it was nothing and if it was something, it was probably just a benign lump and not malignant. She kept telling me that the way the medical assistant told her, it seemed to be severe. I went to Charlton with my mother, and boy they took so long to take her in. I had to leave because, I needed to go to work. My mother understood, and I gave her my cell phone so she could call my grandmother to give her a ride home. I ended up having lunch at the Charlton cafeteria, and went straight to work. At work later in the day I called home, and asked her how it went. She told me it was ok.

A few days later, they called her and advised her to see a surgeon for a breast biopsy. She was all nervous, and depressed. I kept supporting her that maybe it was a benign lump. Although I would tell her that, I wasn't quite sure myself. I was afraid that it was going to be malignant. My father never had any health problems, and in his prospective he didn't believe it was possible. Reality to this was on his back side burner. He kept telling her that it was probably nothing. I remember when I was first diagnosed with Systemic Lupus and when I'd start feeling sick again, he would deny that I was sick, and tell me I was faking it. I still remember those words he told me once when I came home sick,

"You just want attention, and just want to be spoiled."

He'd only believe me when I was stuck in the hospital. Sometimes because of all my health problems, I felt like I was some kind burden to them.

My mother went to see Dr. Felix, and I went with her. She took samples, and told my mother it would take a couple of days for the results. After a couple of days had passed by, on one late evening my mother received a phone call from her doctor. It was malignant! My mother was hysterically crying upstairs in the parlor. My father had come up stairs, and started crying with her. It was one of the worse moments I had experienced in my life. I was ready to tear up crying myself, and could feel the tears come to my eyes. I went downstairs to be with my grandfather that had come and visit us that evening, and cried. My mother then came down arched on my father's shoulders crying as my father told my grandfather that the doctor had called, and that my mother had Breast Cancer. My grandfather held my mother in his arms as if she were his baby girl again, told my mother that she would get through this, and that every thing was going to be ok.

Dr. Felix did another biopsy for more detail in order to specify what kind of cancer, and then she referred my mother to an Oncologist at Saint Anne's Hospital. She then went for this test to see how far the cancer had progressed. Luckily, it was just in her right breast, and was the size of a golf ball. The plan was to do six months of chemotherapy first to kill the cancer cells so it wouldn't progress anymore. Then she'd have to do surgery, and then Radiation. During the first three chemotherapy treatments my mother still worked. She went for her treatments on Friday's so she could have Saturday and Sunday's off to rest. I had suggested that because, I had done chemotherapy myself last year, and also when I was first diagnosed. I knew how intense and potent it was. However, my dose wasn't nearly as strong as the dosages my mother was receiving.

By the fourth treatment, my mother went on short term disability. She had bought herself a wig, and after the fourth treatment her hair was falling in clumps. It was a very difficult moment for her, and I felt so bad. It hurt me to see her so sad. She would show me herself with no wig, and I could see the tears come to her eyes. Every time she did that, I held the tears back. I'd get so heartbroken.

"It's ok, mom. It will grow back when this is all over. Just keep strong! Everything will be ok!" This was all I could say without bursting into tears.

As she progressed to her fifth treatment, she became weaker and more tired. I helped her as much as I could. Most of the time, I'd pickup some groceries she needed, helped her with the cleaning, and the laundry. One day before I left the house to go pick up some milk and eggs for her before I went to work, at the door step she slid her fingers through my hair and thanked me. I could see her eyes getting watery. She almost had me crying. At that moment, I just wanted to hug her and tell her how much I loved her but I felt that if I did, I would end up tearing apart. She was my mother, and I loved her so much.

When chemotherapy was over and she had gone back to work, I went and visit her at the bank on her first day back. I looked at her and smiled. I could see that she was so uncomfortable with the wig on, and looked like she wanted to cry when she saw me. I got so shook up that I wanted to cry myself.

The third time John and I had gone out, Johnny told me that he was thinking of opening his own business. A few minutes later, this man that was sitting at another table close by approached our table, and asked Johnny if he was serious about opening his own business. He gave Johnny his address and phone number, and told Johnny he had a business proposal for him.

Then he turned around, looked at me, and asked Johnny if I was his wife. I was dying to laugh! John looked at me, and both of us started laughing as we told the man no at the same time. Johnny told him we worked together, and we were just friends. However, I would've loved being his wife someday.

After we left the restaurant, we went and took a walk around Buttonwood Park. It felt so good to be with him at the park. I felt so protected, and comfortable. There were two moments when our knuckles brushed against one another and to me, it felt romantic. He told me he was having problems with Carol, and that his parents told him that he should let her go because, she made him so unhappy at times.

I was frank about it. I told him that he should do what he thinks is best for him, and not what his parents think. I told him to do what makes him happy. I wasn't like many girls who would probably just tell him to break up with her just because I loved him that way. I looked at things both ways, and what mattered to me was his happiness.

That night I couldn't sleep either tossing and turning, thinking of him all night. The next morning I woke up singing full of joy. Johnny always brought joy into my heart! He was a great part of my life now, and I felt like I couldn't live without him.

There was another evening he called me, and asked me if I wanted to take a walk around the park. I replied with a yes of course. Those evenings I had spent with him would always be a part of my most precious memories. They were the best times of my life. My heart was always racing and melting at the same time when we were together.

While we walked around the park and talked, I suddenly got those cravings of wanting him so bad. I looked at him while he was walking, and just smiled as I gazed at him. It felt like my feelings were just overflowing. After a moment, he realized I was looking at him and lifted his head. He looked at me and as I turned away, he smiled.

That happened twice that evening, and before we left it seemed like he didn't want to leave. It also seemed like he wanted to tell me something because he was lingering before he left. I wonder what he wanted to say that he didn't have the courage to.

For the rest of the summer, we always kept in touch. I'd write him emails, would go and see him at work, and call him when I could. I got so crazy about him that I started thinking about him more than my own self. My health started declining and seemed to get worse by the minute without me realizing. Besides, I didn't want to believe or admit that I was getting sick again.

I was crazy looking for jobs on online for him, and on the internet all night going to bed around midnight practically every day hoping he'd log on so I could talk with him. I even ignored my praying in which I deeply regretted and asked God for forgiveness. I was so blind and wasn't seeing what I was doing to God, my family and myself. I practically excluded my parents, and the free time I had I would spend it in my room on the computer, waiting to chat with a friend. I guess you could say that I got a bit obsessed with my liking of John. I couldn't help it. I wanted him so much.

A couple of weeks later in October, I started having these sharp pains under my right breast that extended towards my back. The pain was all inside. I tried every remedy I could think of. I tried Ice packs, Ben Gay, muscle heating pads, and I even tried push up bras! One day I even made a joke out of it at work.

"Hey. I found a new remedy for my pain! Push up bras!" I told my friend Pauline. Pauline started laughing. Then a few minutes later, I went up to her as I pretended to be all serious and told her,

"I hope I don't get any scars."

We both started laughing hysterically! That Pauline was a trip. If you wanted to hear a funny joke, you could always count on her! She was an amazing woman as well, fighting diabetes, working, and making a living. She was a sweetheart.

When I finally went to get checked out, the doctor that examined me told me that I probably just pulled a muscle at the gym. It was a pulled muscle, all right! It was no muscle pain. It was the accumulation of fluids in my lungs. However, I didn't know. I thought it was just a pulled muscle like the doctor had told me. I kept trying every remedy I could think of, and also kept treating myself with Ben Gay hoping that it would get better.

A few days later, I had gone by Bradley's Boutique and dropped off an application of Cardi's furniture for John on my lunch break. I left it with Marie, and later that day I called him and asked him if he received the application I left for him.

"I did, Jen. Thank you." He replied.

That day I was in so much pain. I just felt like crying. My whole body was aching, and my right side felt as if it was being continuously stabbed.

After a while before we hung up, Johnny told me something I've always wanted to hear.

"Jen. You're one of the best girls I've ever meant." He told me.

That just melted my soul. I've always wanted to hear that, and hearing it from the man I loved made it even more special to me.

"You're the best guy I've ever meant." I replied as I heard Johnny laughing on the phone.

When we finally hung up, the pain I was enduring seemed to heal from severe to mild. I couldn't believe it! It felt like a miracle. It's amazing what words can do.

Some other weird things happened to me before I became sick, and of course it all had to do with John. For some reason, it seemed like we were always meant to be. One day I walked into work, and I just didn't want to be there. Guess what happened? The first specimen I pick up was named John Arruda. I couldn't help but smile and laugh because, it felt like he was always with me.

One rainy Saturday morning when I woke up, I had no intentions whatsoever to leave the house but, something usual happened. A few minutes later, I felt like going to the bank. I really didn't have to go but I just felt like going, and so I dressed. When I slipped into my car, the impression that I was going to see John and that he was going to need help aroused in my mind. As I came off the exit, I saw John's car stopped on the breakdown lane. I knew it was him because, I could feel it.

I pulled over and when I finally approached his car, I asked him if he needed a ride. He looked mad, and looked like he wanted to cry. He told me he had already called triple A. I felt so bad for him, and kept him company for a while. Before I left, as I walked to my car I stared at him. I was craving to kiss him before I left, and tell him that everything was going to be all right. Later that night, I wrote him an email.

Hey Johnny,   *9/15/05*

How are you? I hope things are getting better for you! You deserve the best! All I want is for you to be happy John, and as a girl who loved you so much I did as much as I could to make you smile and laugh! Every time you'd laugh or smile, you'd spark the flame.

The reason I'm writing you this letter is because, I'm breaking up the going out together. I know you maybe saying "Gee, she knows I have so many problems right now and she has to give me another headache" but, I had to end it. I just never had the courage to. I loved going out with you John but, every time I would go out with you I'd get so attached, and end up thinking about you all the time. It's not right for your girlfriend and it's not right for me either because, no matter how much I would try to hide my feelings, I wanted much more than just friendship.

I don't know if you noticed but sometimes I'd try to hide what I felt for you because, I knew you couldn't give me what I really wanted. Like on your birthday when you asked me what I was thinking about? Well at that moment, I was craving to be in your arms and give you a happy birthday kiss. And like today when your car broke down, before I left I was craving to give you a kiss. And you know every time I'd try not to think of you, I would always encounter you or would see something that would remind me of you.

I love you, Johnny and don't want to hurt you in any way. It's just that going out together is not helping me move on with my feelings. It spikes it up. Those were the happiest times of my life when it was just the two of us. You'll make a good husband to any girl Johnny.

As for your girlfriend, she doesn't deserve to someday find out that her boyfriend is going out with another girl besides her. It's a small world John. I know that I wouldn't like it if I had a boy-friend who went out with another girl besides me.

You'll always be my best friend Johnny but, I can't go out with you anymore. No matter how much I want to. I hope I didn't hurt you, Johnny. I just can't control my feelings like I used to. It's been two years that I've been in love, and I can't keep dreaming about something that's not possible. Sorry to write you such a long letter but, I had to explain myself! As friends we'll always keep in touch! Take care!

Your friend

Jenny Jen

12

My Enemy Calls

A few days later, I found out that John and Carol broke up. They broke up on the same day his car broke down, and the same day I wrote him that letter. So what do I do? What do you think I did?

I ended up going to Bradley's Boutique but, I didn't see him and so I told one of the girls up front to tell him I was there. When I walked out the door and was walking to my car, I heard someone yell out "Jenny Jen." It was my sweetheart! I told him I was sorry to hear about what happened between him and his girlfriend, and we ended up talking for a while.

A couple of days after, I went and see him again. I stood a good long hour or so talking with him in the security cubicle. He told me what Carol was like most of the time. Nothing like my cousin had told me. It seemed to me that she was just interested in what Johnny could give her. If Johnny were my boyfriend, I could careless in how much he could buy me. All I would want from him would be his love, and nothing else.

He looked so pale, and had his arm around his waist while he was sitting down. I felt so bad, and hurt to see him hurt. I really wanted to hug him at that moment. However, I was a bit timid because I didn't know if he at that moment hated all women because of what happened. I did the best I could to cheer him up. I also reminded him of all the good times we had together. After a while, he looked at me and smiled for the first time that day.

"Yeah. We had a fun time together." He told me.

I was glad I made him smile. After a while he started telling me, "I guess I'll just become single for the rest of my life."

That made me so mad! Here I was waiting so anxiously to be his, and he turns around and tells me this! I then replied,

"What are you talking about? There are plenty of girls out there that love you!"

Then I stopped for a moment to gain the courage to tell him what I've always wanted to tell him face to face,

"I love you." I could feel my heart sink. I didn't know how he was going to react.

"I really appreciate it." He told me.

I totally understood that he was going through a tough moment right now, and didn't want to hear about the word of love but, I felt the need to tell him how I felt in person. I couldn't hold it in any longer, especially after he told me that!

Every week I'd go to the Oncology Center to get Neulasta and Procrit injections to boost my white and red cell count because, my blood counts were all declining. The Celcept immunosuppressant my doctor put me on wasn't helping me. It was just decreasing my white count. I told my doctor this plenty of times, and I wanted her to take me off the medication but, she insisted that I should be on it. I didn't know what to think anymore. All I knew was that I was getting worse by the minute. My sharp pains just kept intensifying.

I was supposed to go to the Oncology Center every week after my last chemotherapy treatment but, there was one week I felt too tired to go and didn't go. Well, I suffered the consequences. The following week when I went, my white count was extremely low, and my doctor ordered me to stay out of work because I was too weak. A few days later, I went for more blood work and still felt horrible. I could barely move because, I was in so much pain. While I was there, I requested to go to the emergency room. Although my parents didn't want to believe I was sick, I was glad I did go to the emergency room. While I was there, my parents kept telling me,

"Oh, you have nothing. You're just faking it for attention. It seems like you enjoy being in the hospital." Both my mother and father kept scolding me until the doctor finally came in with the chest x-ray results.

Maybe they just didn't want to believe that I was having another major flare. I wouldn't lie to them about a health condition. Why would I do that? I'm such a live person who loves to go to the extreme, and who loves being energetic. I would never pick up a sick role over an energetic role. I was very hurt as they kept nagging me. They couldn't even trust their own daughter. I know when I'm sick. I feel it in my body, and at that moment I was feeling it everywhere. It felt as if I were being stabbed with a thousand knives all over my body. I couldn't even move because with every sudden move I felt so much pain.

Sure enough they kept me because, I had a touch of pneumonia and my lungs were filled with fluids. I kept telling the doctors that my sickness was causing all of this but, they kept looking for infection. I'd get so mad. They thought that because I was a Medical Lab Tech, I was trying to be smart but the truth was that I knew my stuff, and I knew my case more than any doctor that was there because I lived with it.

After a week or so, I had asked my grandmother to pick me up a wrap from Subway because, the nurse told me I could have whatever I wanted. That day I was already having shortness of breath, and as I was eating the sub, I could feel it get worse and worse until I couldn't breathe anymore. I told my grandmother to call the nurse immediately. In a few seconds, I blacked out. I didn't know where I was, and what was happening. I had gone through congestive heart failure due to a leaky mitral valve in my heart that had gone from moderate to severe. They put me in the ICU where they suck a urinary catheter up my urethra which was so painful. I cried so hard. Then they kept puncturing me to find a vein, in order to start an IV. I kept grasping the sheets with all my strength as tears came down my eyes while they probed back and forth to find a vein. They put me on five liters of oxygen. My arms were all bruised for them always probing to find a vein. I'd cry as I looked at my black and blue arms.

"Why didn't they just nail me to a cross? For Christ's sake!"

Then I went to the CCU and all those floors at Charlton. All of the nurses already knew me, and would ask me:

"You're still here?"

After a while, I started filling up with fluids everywhere. There was a moment when I was on the ICU that I was nearly unconscious. I suffered every prick and every probe while I was there besides my condition. I could barely breathe, talk or walk.

After a good month at Charlton, I just wanted to go home. When I wasn't as swollen with fluids as before, they sent me home and advised me to keep my feet elevated most of the time. When I arrived home, I had made arrangements to go back to work and go on with my life but, the worse was yet to come.

Although I couldn't stand up for long periods of time, the first day I was ok I had to sit in the shower to wash up because, I'd get out of breath and would get too tired standing up. The second day I couldn't even sleep at night. I woke up at three in the morning, and couldn't breathe laying down. As I sat up on my bed, I wept silently.

"I'm too young to die, Lord." I cried.

"I have many things I want to experience in this world, Lord! Please don't end my life! I want to have a chance to experience that first kiss. I want to be here to help others and my family." I wept.

That morning it grew worse. Even sitting up, I would get out of breath. I asked my mother to bring me to the emergency room because, I knew if I hadn't gone that moment I probably wouldn't have made it through the night.

When I arrived, the doctors knew my case because I was there a few days ago. They immediately took care of me. Again they kept puncturing and probing to find a vein, as I let out painful cries.

"When is this going to end?" I cried.

I felt horrible knowing that my mother was sick too, and that I couldn't to be with her to help her. She kept telling me to not worry about her but, to worry about myself. She told me to keep fighting because she needed me.

I loved her so much. I don't know how I could do without her. She kept giving me hopes that I'd break though all of this, and was always there when I was facing the worst moments of my life.

My blood pressure was sky high, and I was going through congestive heart failure for a second time. The doctor in the emergency room suggested that I be transferred to Mass General, one of the biggest hospitals where they had doctors from all over the world. At that hospital they specialized mostly with heart conditions, and they wanted to send me up there for open heart surgery to replace my leaky mitral valve. My mother didn't want me to go because, she wouldn't be able to see me every day. Boston was like a two-hour drive from Swansea with traffic but, I told her that I would be fine and would call her every day. I also alerted her that I had to do what was best for me. She understood, and that night I went by ambulance to Mass General. Before I had gone, the nurse had given me some morphine to make me have a good trip but, I ended up throwing up all the way there.

When I was wheeled out of the ambulance, I was so amazed in how big the hospital was. It had twenty-three floors! Imagine that! I was on the sixteenth floor, and had a nice view of the Charles River. It was so nice at night to just gaze at the window, and see all the different color lights from various buildings of all different shapes and sizes. Although I was on bed rest, it was one way to drift me away from my health issues. The nurses were very pleasant, and made me feel comfortable. The nurse in charge of me, alerted me that I would be seeing a bunch of doctors in the morning.

The next morning I saw a couple of doctors like the nurse had said. They all told me I was one strong woman to fight all of this. I had seen a Cardiologist, Rheumatologist, and a Nephrologist. They all told me that they would join together to create a plan to determine the best way to treat me because, my case was difficult. I was in congestive heart failure, and was borderline towards renal failure. Each one asked me a series of questions. I was so sick of them asking me the same questions over and over again. The Rheumatologist suggested that putting the Lupus in remission before any kind of heart surgery would be the best approach, and so the Nephrologist suggested trying this new drug called Celcept on me which my original Nephrologist had tried me on and didn't seem to work. I told him it didn't work on me but, he thought I was just trying to be smart. He encouraged me to try it and told me that they'd keep an eye on my white count. My cardiologist tried me on so many blood pressure medications, and after about a week found the right medication for me.

My Nephrologist that idiot, started me on a very high dose of Celcept. He put me on 1000mg, combined with the twenty something medications I was taking. I was getting intoxicated with all these drugs, and would get the chills, headaches, and throw up. My stomach couldn't hold anything because, it was so intoxicated. One day while I was having breakfast, I blacked out. Luckily a nurse walked in, in enough time before I fell off the hospital bed. Like I say, God always keeps an angel my way when I need help. The Nephrologist told me that he couldn't understand why I couldn't handle all the medications I was taking if all his patients could handle it. I turned around and said,

"Well. Look at my size. I'm a very small person, and there's only so much my body can handle."

"Well. I guess I can take that into consideration." He told me after thinking it through.

No Dah … What kind of doctor was he. Common sense. It seemed like some of these doctors didn't know the difference between a melon and a watermelon. So much education I don't know what for.

He ended up cutting my dosage to 500mg like my original Nephrologist had done. The other doctors staggered my medications so I won't take a whole load at once. They were going to preform open heart surgery on me but because my kidneys were shutting down, they ended up putting me on dialysis in order to clear the toxins out of my blood. After one day of dialysis, they pulled the catheter out. I had a funny feeling that once wasn't going be enough. And sure enough I was right. Now they weren't concentrating on my heart but, my kidneys. My Nephrologist told me to my face that he could guarantee me 99% that my kidneys weren't going to survive. I cried so much that day. It was clear that he had no feelings in what he said to me. I felt like telling him,

"Are you God to make that 99% assumption?"

That day I called my mother crying, and told her what the doctor had told me. She was so mad that she called my Nephrologist up there, and told him that he had no right to approach me that way.

"You're not God!" She told him.

They tried keeping me dry so I wouldn't fill up with fluids again, and it reached to a point when they were drying me out too much. I was on a no salt, cardiac and renal diet. Plus, a fluid restriction diet. I would get frustrated because, everything I liked and loved eating I couldn't eat. My mouth was always so dry, and the only remedies I had for it were popsicles, which would make me thirsty, ice chips, and these green swabs soaked in water. I felt like I was a pregnant woman with ice chips always in my mouth.

One night my mouth was so terribly dry that I couldn't sleep and so, I called the nurse and asked her for a popsicle. There weren't any near by so, she called the cafeteria and had someone come up. I only had asked for one but instead, the guy from the cafeteria brought me five. I ate one out of the two that were in the package, and tried to call the nurse so she could take the one left over that I held in my hand plus the other four. I kept pressing the nurse button. However, the nurse never answered my call. An hour or so had passed, and still no answer. The popsicle was already melting down my hand, and no nurse to help me. I was so tired and frustrated that I just started crying. Then I got so mad that I flung the popsicle towards the nicely painted white wall in front of me, which made a lovely red painting. A few minutes later, my mother called me. I told her that I had paged the nurse, and no one had answered my call. My mother called the nurses station, and they found out that my room had lost connection to the nursing station.

At those moments any little thing would agitate me because I was suffering so much. I was always hurting everywhere and always so tired. Tired of bring tortured with needles, and catheters. Tired of reasoning with my doctors that I was right about telling them that all of this was due to my sickness. I felt hopeless because I wasn't seeing myself getting better but worse. I was so sick of being in the hospital, and was so sick of being sick.

They ended up switching me to another room. I was getting so sick of the doctors up there. They weren't doing, or resolving anything for me. The only thing they accomplished on me was finding the right heart, and blood pressure medications. One day was so mad and told my nurse,

"I want to speak with my doctor, and I want to speak to him now. I don't care if you have to page him but, I want to speak to him now."

The nurse saw how frustrated and angry I was. They weren't doing anything for me besides trying all sorts of drugs on me. I felt like I was some kind of science project. When my primary care physician came, I told him,

"I'd like to be transferred back to Charlton. It's closer to home, and I'll be able to see my family every day. Besides, no one is doing anything for me up here, and I feel like I'm some kind of science project. I can get my kidneys treated at Charlton the same way I'd get treated here. I want to go back, and if I need a doctor's approval I'll get you one." I told him.

Sure enough, the next day they had my discharge paperwork ready. Before I left, I apologized to them because it wasn't their fault that much wasn't accomplished. They tried the best they could. My case wasn't easy. They understood that I was just frustrated because, of being in the hospital for so long and that I just wanted to be next to my family.

The next day I headed back to Charlton. That night I asked one of the nurses I knew since I had been admitted for a favor. I had written a letter that I wanted her to email John because, I knew that he must have been worried about me by now. I always talked to John one way or another but since I was in the hospital, I hadn't talked to any friends besides Beth O. and Dottie that came and visit me. Only my coworkers and family knew I was in the hospital. No one else did. There was no time anyway because, I was always in critical condition. As the nurse read the letter I wrote him, she began to cry.

Johnny! It's Jenny Jen! I've been going through hell!

Johnny! On October 28, I was admitted because my sickness flared up again, and this time it's much worse than the last flare. I've been in the hospital for three months now between Charlton, and Mass General fighting for my life. I've faced Congestive heart failure several times, and am now facing Kidney failure. They're talking about open heart surgery, and terminal dialysis! I'm a mess Johnny, and I'm in so much pain right now that you can't even imagine! I can barely talk because they've been keeping me dry, and I'm on bed rest because I can barely breathe when I walk. I've been suffering every prick, puncture and every probe that's been afflicted to my body. Sometimes I feel as if I were getting nailed to a cross. For Christ's sake! I don't know how much more of this I can take. I'm tired of fighting for my life. I'm exhausted. I'm sick of being sick! I want to be that happy girl I was before.

I miss you, Johnny! I miss you so much. I hope I can get through all of this so I can see you again, and be that happy girl I've always been. You're one of the reasons why I want to live Johnny. I love you.

Sincerely,

Jenny Jen

I was supposed to start long term dialysis while I was still at the hospital but, my doctor told me they wanted to hold off and keep me dry to see how my kidneys would respond. I was at Charlton for another three weeks or so recuperating and practicing how to walk again because, I was on bed rest for so long.

If it wasn't for Prima Care whom had paid their part in order for me to get health insurance, I would've been in so much debt. Besides, I wasn't eligible for insurance yet because I was still on my three month probation. They kept my job and were so understanding.

When they finally sent me home after a total of three months in hospitals, my mother and I went to the pharmacy to pick up my medications. I picked up thirty prescriptions that day, and ended up with a two hundred-dollar co-pay for a month supply.

While we were waiting, I checked my cell phone for any messages and to my surprise, John had left me a voice mail. He was worried about me. I tried calling him but, he had his cell phone off and so I ended up leaving a voice mail.

"Johnny. I miss you. I've been through hell these past months fighting for my life. I'm sorry I couldn't get in touch with you sooner but, I wasn't capable of doing anything for a while. I love you, Johnny. I will always love you." I said as I felt little rhinestones of tears sliding down my puffy cheeks.

I wasn't capable of driving and I could barely walk or talk but, I begged my parents to bring me by Bradley's Boutique because I wanted to see my friends and most of all, I wanted to see John again.

My mouth was so dry that I could barely speak but, I made the efforts to talk with my friends and tell them what was going on. After a while I noticed John waiting patiently as always for me to come up to him and talk with him. I could tell he was sad to see me so sick. When I went up to him, I automatically gave him a hug and began crying.

"I missed you, honey. I missed you so much." I whispered into his earlobe.

He was one of the reason's I wanted to live for.

After about a week I went to see my Nephrologist. My skin had a yellowish tinge to it and by the looks of me, you could tell that I was still very ill. Inside I felt horrible, lifeless, and very tired. My blood work wasn't any good, and so doctor told me,

"Jen. I'm afraid you're going to need terminal hemodialysis. Your kidneys are not responding."

My doctor scheduled an appointment for me to see a vascular surgeon, in order for them to place a direct access for me to undergo hemodialysis. At Charlton they gave me local anesthetics, and placed a catheter that connected to a major artery and draped down the right side of my chest with two valves at the end. After the procedure, I stood at the hospital over night, and did a session of dialysis there. Then when I was discharged again, they referred me to an Artificial Kidney Center in Fall River.

Although my doctor told me dialysis was terminal until a transplant was in line for me, in my mind I always thought dialysis was only going to be temporary, and that by one week or two I'd be off of it like I did when I had my major flare in the Azores. However, this time I wasn't so lucky.

A week had passed by, and I was still doing dialysis. Dialysis its self was very tiresome. I'd sit there on a recliner for three hours and a half feeling crappy and lightheaded. My blood pressure would fluctuate from highs to lows in just a few seconds, and sometimes I'd throw up because I'd get so sick to my stomach. After the treatment I always felt so crappy and tired. All I wanted was to lie down and rest. I went three times a week and dreaded every time I had to go because, I knew that it would just suck out all my energy that was reserved for that day.

At home I couldn't even walk up a flight of stairs because, with any little exertion I'd get out of breath and my heart would race. I felt as if I were an old lady with such a youthful soul. After a month of dialysis, I realized that this was going to be permanent until a donor was available. I became so disgusted with myself, and fell into a big depression. I was mad, frustrated, and just didn't want to accept the fact that I had to do dialysis for a living. I felt like my life was ruined, and that I was never going to be what I was before. I was never going to be that energized, multi task girl I was who always kept herself fit, and would always be there to help anyone anywhere. I had nothing to look forward to, except feeling sick all the time.

"What's the point of living if all I'm ever going to do is suffer, and make my family suffer?"

I'd tell myself.

My depression made me feel sicker than what I actually was. I started rejecting myself from overcoming and defeating my disease. There were even days I thought of suicide and thought to myself,

"What's the point of me living if I'm never going to have a normal life, and don't have anything to look forward to?"

I was bringing myself down. I omitted myself from everyone, and just wanted to be alone all the time. I wasn't there for my mother at that time when she needed me the most after surgery because, I just had no desire in living.

After a month dwelling on such a deep depression, I sat on my bed in the middle of the night, and talked with God,

"God, how can I live like this! I feel crappy every single day, and my life is down to nothing. Tell me! How can I live like this? Show me a way to get through this, and show me a way to fight all of this."

That next morning as I looked in the mirror while combing my hair, I told myself,

"This is not I! This is not I! I'm a fighter, not a loser. I'm needed by many people and can't just throw my life away because, of all my problems. I want to live for God, my family, for Johnny and for all those who love me."

From that day on I started picking up the pieces of my life again. I started driving again, and went back to work part-time working twenty hours. It was very difficult for me to do dialysis, and then later in the day go to work. After my dialysis treatments, I'd come home, and sleep until it was time for me to go to work. It was still very hard on me, but God always carried me along.

It was strange for me to be in public again because, I had been isolated between being in hospitals and being at home for such a long time. I just wanted to be myself again like I was before but, I felt different and awkward. I was always afraid I wasn't that same person in the eyes of others like I was before. I just felt strange. After a month or so passed by, I picked up where I left off and finally felt like my own little self again.

Later on I gradually started picking up my thirty-two hours with my manager's and doctor's approval, and still did dialysis three times a week. I don't know how I did it but, to me there is only one answer. It was God who helped me with every step I took. He saw that I was trying to help myself, and so he gave me a hand.

Stephen, our courier was so happy to see me back. He told me,

"Jen. I'm so glad you're back. I missed you. It was lonely without you here!"

That made me feel so good, and so special. All my other co-workers then turned around and told me that what he said was true, and that I was of great lose to them. I felt so loved.

Stephen was a nice guy. He was such a good-hearted person, and that was what made him so special. He was like a brother to me. On days when I felt crappy, just one of his smiles would make me feel so much better. He had a gift. One day he asked me about my condition and wanted me to talk with a friend of his because, she had a son who needed a kidney and she could probably help me. He was such a good friend.

John and I hadn't gone out for the longest time since I was sick, and I missed him so much. I'd think about him quite often, and always wondered how he was doing. Sometimes I'd talk to him on the internet, or write him emails but, it was never the same. I was always dying to see him. I longed for him. However, I knew what I was doing was right because he didn't love me that way. There was always a war between my heart and my mind. My heart wanted him so much, and my mind kept telling me to do the right thing. I tried everything I could think of to erase him from my heart but, it seemed like my feelings for him were just crazy glued to my heart because nothing would work.

My friend Terri popped up online one night, and asked me how was doing. Then she asked me if I wanted to have lunch some where. I was delighted with the idea because I hadn't seen her in such a long time. Then she told me,

"Maybe we should invite John to come too. I think he'd like that."

I was trying to avoid going out with John because, I knew he never wanted anything serious with me. I've tried so hard to avoid myself from falling back into him, and now she had totally broke my wings. I still loved him so much.

I told Terri that it would be nice to see him again. When the day came for us to go out, Terri called me and told me she couldn't go. I was upset. Now it wasn't I between Terri and John but, just John and I by ourselves. After a moment I thought,

"Well, he's still by his lonesome. Maybe there's still a chance for me to win his heart."

That day I got all decked out to impress him, and that day instead of impressing him I ended up getting slapped in the face with the notice that he was seeing another girl. As soon as he told me, I just wanted to leave. I felt as if my heart was stabbed, and all I wanted to do was cry with so much pain. I was mad for a while but, then I realized that I knew along that he didn't like me that way. But why? What did I lack? What was missing in me that he liked in other girls? Was I not good enough for him? Was I that hard to fall in love with? In one way, I was glad that he told me the truth. However, I knew that this was going to be the last time I'd see him again.

I wished he had told me from the very beginning how he felt. It would have caused much less heart ache.

My Aunt Nancy and my cousin Melanie tried to see if they were matches for me but, no luck. I have a lot to thank God for having these two brave women who were willing to donate a kidney to me in order to give me my life back. My aunt and my cousin had shown how much they wanted to help me, and I hope they know that this sacrifice they were willing to comply with, will always be within my heart as a sign of their love for me. I love them both with all my heart, and want them to always know that I'll be here for anything they need. My heart goes out to them.

I had many people tell me that they'd donate a kidney to me if I needed one but, none of them besides my cousin and aunt had courage to when that time came. Even family members told me this but, it was only a bunch of words. I would have rather them not tell me anything, than keeping my hopes up thinking I'd get a transplant soon.

I had been on dialysis for a year now and was just waiting. One morning I received a letter from Bristol Community College telling me that I had been accepted in the nursing program. I was happy about it but, was worried at the same time. How was I going to manage doing dialysis, working and going to school? I kept asking the Lord,

"How am I going to do this, Lord?"

Well. Miracles do happen. A few weeks before nursing started for me, and a few days before Christmas, my kidneys miraculously improved and kept on improving. My doctors couldn't believe it. I had End Stage Renal Failure, and was now with almost all my kidney function back. They took me off dialysis a few days before Christmas, and I felt the difference. I was much more energetic, and alert like old times. I had quite a few scars and bruises on my body that didn't heal completely but, what mattered to me was that I was still alive.

Once my sickness was stable once again, I had done some research on the internet about my disease. After this flare, I just wanted to take care of myself as best as I could so I would never have to face another major flare in my life again. With my luck, I found an article that was very easy to read, and had caught my eye. (Poore, R.(2006) Lupus *(Systemic Lupus Erythematosus)* Retrieved June 20, 2006)

"There are three types of Lupus. They're called Systemic Lupus Erythematosus, Discoid or Cutaneous Lupus, and Drug-induced Systemic Lupus.

Systemic Lupus Erythematosus also known as (SLE), is the most life-threatening type of Lupus. It attacks a person's internal organs such as the heart, lungs, kidneys, and sometimes a person's cental nervous system. Discoid or Cutaneous Lupus is not as life threatening and serious as (SLE). It triggers a person's skin rather than a person's organs. Patients with this type of Lupus, develop severe rashes, and skin sores. Drug-Induced Systemic Lupus is caused by certain types of medication and is only temporary. When the person stops the medication, signs and symptoms of Lupus disappear. It is systemic and does attack one's own tissue but, to a much lesser extent as (SLE).Doctors haven't yet discovered the particular cause of this disease. However, they strongly believe that people with Lupus are born with certain genes that effect how the immune system functions. There are also a number of things that can trigger Lupus such as, viral infections, bacterial infections, stress, and the sun.

There are also a number of signs and symptoms a patient with Lupus can watch for that indicate that a flare has begun.

• **Fatigue**—People with Lupus complain of extreme tiredness.

- **Skin Conditions**—Many people with Lupus develop skin rashes when a flare is about to happen. One familiar rash that is commonly noted is the "Butterfly Rash." Other warning signs include, skin sores, sores in the mouth or on the lips.

- **Sunlight**—Sunlight triggers Lupus flares, and those who have fair skin are more prone to a flare if out in the sun too long.

- **Central Nervous System**—Lupus may affect a person's nervous system by causing depression, constant headaches, and anxiety.

- **Joint and Muscle Pain**—People with Lupus complain of muscle and joint pain. Joints sometimes are swollen and warm. Lupus usually triggers, the wrists, hands, ankles, knees and elbows.

- **Heart Condition**—Lupus can cause inflammation on the lining of the heart sac, and also heart murmurs.

- **Fever**—People with Lupus tend to have low-grade fevers when a flare is about to occur.

- **Weight loss**—People loss weight when a Lupus flare is being brought on because they have a loss of appetite.

- **Swollen Glands and Hair Loss**—Many people with Lupus experience hair loss during a Lupus episode, and most people have swollen glands when Lupus is in its active stage.

Doctors usually treat Lupus by having patients use corticosteroid cremes for rashes, take non steroidal anti-inflammatory drugs (NSAIDs) such as; (Acetaminophen, and Ibuprofen) for fever, joint and muscle pain, and take oral corticosteroids such as, (Prednisone) to keep the disease under control. However, corticosteroids are very powerful and can cause terrible side effects. Some of the major side effects are usually weight gain, stomach ulcers, and decreased immunity to fight infection. Because of this, doctors try to keep patients at a minimal dose to reduce side effects and still keep the disease under control but, sometimes doctors don't have a choice because in some cases the sickness is too advanced.

Much more females get Lupus than males. Lupus is also mainly seen in Asian, and African-American people. It usually occurs between ages 15 thru 45, and is usually hereditary. Lupus can be controlled by patients getting enough rest, limiting stress loads, avoiding the sun by wearing sun screen at all times and protective clothing, not smoking, exercising regularly to prevent fatigue and joint stiffness, and by being familiar with the signs and symptoms of the disease.

Despite these facts about the disease, many patients with Lupus develop many complications such as; pregnancy issues, blood disorders, heart and kidney problems, and nervous system problems. Many people with Lupus can live a normal life but, usually need to reduce their activity level, and stress load in order to keep the disorder quiescent. In all, Systemic Lupus Erythematosus is the most life threatening disease. Many deaths of young adults with Lupus are caused by the disease attacking their internal organs causing damage and failure. Newer medications have come out and have improved the lives of those like me whom suffer from this disease. However, a cure hasn't been found yet. (Poore, R.(2006) Lupus *(Systemic Lupus Erythematosus)* Retrieved June 20, 2006)"

Despite all the research my mother and I had done on my disease, living with it was want taught my parents and I how severe and life threatening this disease truly was.

On July of 2006 my mother's friend's granddaughter was diagnosed with leukemia.

"I thought I was bad! What about that 3-year old little girl. She's in much worse shape than I was." I told myself.

One day I went by the bank where my mother worked and Carol, the grandmother of that little girl, was distributing flyers with her picture for a bone marrow donation drive that was set up for her. I took some and put one at my job, and some at doctor's offices. When I went back into my car, I felt as if something had touched me to go leave one at the church rectory. I listened to it, and dropped one off. When I went back into my car, I felt as if God at that moment had touched me and restored me with so much happiness because as I drove home, I kept singing, smiling and laughing for no reason. A few months later, a donor was available for that child and when I found out, that made me so happy.

It was sad to see me suffer so much but, it was even sadder to see a 3-year-old suffer with leukemia. There is always worst out there. You can never say that no one's ever suffered like you because, there will always be someone out there who is going through much worse.

When I started nursing, I felt like this was the start of a new life. In the beginning of the semester, it wasn't as hard as people would tell me but, later in the semester it became harder, and harder. Working twenty-four hours wasn't helping either. However, I needed a job. What would kill me, were all of the chapters I had to read. Besides, Monday's we'd go research our patient's at the hospital after class coming home at three o'clock in the evening, and then we had to write up a ten to fifteen page care plan for our patient. We had to research patient's medical diagnosis, medications, and come up with nursing interventions.

It would take me hours to get it done. Besides, every thing had to be fully detailed. Sometimes I wished I had more time to finish it for the next morning but, there were never enough hours in the day. There were times when I'd get all uptight, and would cry in front of my computer. My mother kept telling me that if it was too much for me, then she suggested me to drop out. She warned me that stress wasn't good for my sickness, and she was right but that's not what I wanted. I felt like God wanted me to become a nurse. Sometimes I'd talk to my friends on the phone, and just that made me lift my spirit up again.

When my friend Katie from my nursing class had come into the picture, I felt kind of iffy around her. She was sort of popular because, she became president of the class. Sometimes she never stopped bragging about her so-called Johnny who lived with her. Guess what I was thinking?

"Is this the Katie John was talking about?" I questioned myself.

For a while I didn't know how to react, and kept rolling my eyes every time she talked about her so-called Johnny hoping she'd specify her relationship a bit more. After a week or so I caught her saying "My husband Johnny." Boy! I had felt so much better after that. Katie was actually a very nice person. We became best friends, and helped each other with studying. One day while we were studying, for the hell of it I broke out laughing.

"Why are you laughing, Jenny?" She looked at me with a smile.

"I'm laughing because when I first meant you, I thought you were the Katie that one of my best friends is going out with. You were always bragging about your Johnny, and I thought it was the same Johnny I know."

"No. Anyway if he was, why were you hesitating to talk with me in the beginning? I saw you rolling your eyes when you'd look at me." Katie started laughing.

I was all red, and for the first time I had opened up to a friend. I told her how I felt and how hard it's been to move on. She was someone I could trust. I knew she'd keep it to herself.

Despite the fact that I was mad about how it ended, I still loved John so much. Every time I'd enter his name on my log in screen at work, it reminded me of him, and of all the good times we had together.

Although my nursing semester was hard, it was also fun. Our clinical group was our family. Katie, Chelsea, Kelly, Jennifer, Kayla,

Joyce, and Gabriella were in my clinical group and boy we were a fun bunch. We helped each other while we were in clinical and in lab. We also created a study group. Later in the semester Kayla and Gabriella dropped out which upset the rest of the group because, we had already created that friendship bond. Anyway, I had passed the semester, and was now looking forward to the next semester which was about Obstetrics and Pediatrics.

This new phlebotomist came to work with us. His name was Pedro. He was originally from St. Michael's, Azores and of course has his accent. He was good looking I have to admit, and had such a nice smile. I took me a while to know him but when I did, I found out that he was a very sweet and thoughtful person.

After a while we became good friends. Sometimes he'd ask me to pick up coffee, and when I'd come back, he'd smile and tell me I was the best. After while I knew his recipe by heart. He didn't have to tell me because, I knew that it was always a medium extra, extra. He had a sweet tooth I must say. As the months passed by, I started getting a crush on him. I liked when he'd play around with me, and scare the heck out of me on Saturday's when I was all alone in the back.

"Jenny!" He'd call me in a high pitch.

It was always so quiet in the back on Saturdays, with the exception of the analyzers. Sometimes I'd be thinking about things, and then he'd startle me.

"Did I scare you?" He'd ask. Then smile.

"Yeah." I'd laugh.

Pedro was a nice man. He deserved to someday find a nice person who would take care of him and his son and bring love and happiness to both for the rest of their lives.

I started playing around with him. Sometimes I'd send him a fax.

Pedro,

You're the best! Keep smiling! Mini-Me

And sometimes, I'd put a smiley sticker in the back of his jacket.

He had shown me that John wasn't the only one I'd make smile but, him too. Sometimes I'd surprise him with a coffee, and sometimes he'd buy me a coffee and tell me it was on him. Pedro had such a good heart. He was such a caring and loving person. Even patients bragged about him, and would bring him pastry as a sign of their appreciation. I knew someone like him could make me love again but, I was afraid to love another man like I've loved John. It was too painful to realize at the end that the man you loved for so long wasn't meant for you.

I'm not going to let anything ruin my life anymore. I will defeat sickness, and this time let the man of my dreams whom ever he may be find me, and not vice versa. It doesn't work that way. At least for me it didn't. All I know is that when I find that Mr. Right who comes by and steals my heart, my loneliness will be no more and instead, happiness will come knocking at my door.

Since I was sick this last time, I've become a strong woman. I've learned how to value my life and myself. I live and appreciate each day of my life to the fullest, and flourish my live and loving spirit to everyone.

All I want now is to find my happiness. Sometimes I feel like God wants more of me. I feel that he wants me to be someone important like a doctor but, all I really want is to become a nurse, get married, and be a wonderful wife and mother someday. I just want to have a normal life like everyone else, and be loved. I deserve to be loved after all that I've been through. I deserve every bit of happiness this world has to offer me. I know there is worst out there, and I give a lot of credit to those who suffer like me or worse. They deserve to be happy too, and live a normal and healthy life.

Life will never be a river of roses, and some may struggle more than others. For some people when a little challenge comes into their life, they just want to give up, and lose hope but, look at me! I've been through so much, and yet have never totally given up hope. When I was on terminal dialysis I was about to give up but, I knew deep down inside that wasn't I. That wasn't my type of person or my personality. I've always been a fighter. At that point in my life, I had been to so much and felt like it was never going to end but, it did and hopefully for good.

My message to everyone is that no matter how hard the road may get, always fight for your happiness, and your life. Make the best of each day, and live each day to the fullest because life is too short and besides, we never know what tomorrow will bring. Most of all, never fail to smile. One smile can cure so much if you just believe!

All I know is that no matter how hard and narrow my journey may get, I will fight for what I want in this world and will keep climbing the ladder to success until that day when my prince calls for me. I won't let anything bother me, and when my enemy calls, I'll defeat every bit of it and let it know that I am stronger.

Reference List

Wallace, D. J. MD.(1995). *The Lupus Book.* New York, Oxford: Oxford University Press

Poore, R.(2006) Lupus *(Systemic Lupus Erythematosus)* Retrieved June 20, 2006, from http://body.aol.com/conditions/lupus-systemic-lupus-erythematosus

978-0-595-43281-3
0-595-43281-6

CPSIA information can be obtained at www.ICGtesting.com
Printed in the USA
BVOW07s1636250914

368345BV00001B/1/P